sensational SOUTACHE

JEWELRY MAKING

braided jewelry techniques for 15 statement pieces

CSILLA PAPP

INTERWEAVE.
interweave.com

CINCINNATI, OHIO

contents

the projects

introduction

SOUTACHE IS A DECORATIVE BRAID; it is colorful, yet at the same time, it can be amazingly monochromatic. It's extraordinarily light, luxurious and stylish. Not to fall in love with a technique using this wonderful material is simply impossible. Soutache embroidery doesn't require much planning ahead. It almost doesn't matter what kind of pearl, stone, crystal or other materials you use—the result is always amazing.

When I first came across a piece of jewelry made with soutache, I went online to look for information about the technique, but I discovered that details were elusive. As a result, I've learned almost everything I know about the technique on my own. I bought some soutache braids and slowly began to figure out the steps. I practiced a lot and eventually progressed to more difficult projects. At first, I felt that even four hands would not be enough to master the technique, but I didn't give up.

In time, I developed my design style. I am often inspired by nature, and I find plenty of inspiration in fashion designers' collections as well. My designs are modern, youthful and vibrant. I love playing with colors in my designs—the color combinations of soutache braids are endless.

In this book, I will show you how interesting and varied soutache embroidery can be. First I'll teach you the basic techniques that you'll need to have a good understanding of soutache embroidery. Then you'll learn to create fifteen projects, including bracelets, earrings, brooches, rings and necklaces. I've designed each to be a source of ideas and inspiration, giving you the opportunity to advance your skills. With the techniques you'll learn throughout this book, there's no limit to where your imagination can take you.

Some projects, like the Zima Earrings (page 32) or Baroque Bracelet (page 42), will be very simple, while others, like the India Choker (page 90), will challenge you.

You don't have to follow the instructions precisely, as you might have a different stone available or you may want to try alternate colors. Go for it! I encourage you to let your imagination run free. Soutache is the kind of art where you can feel free to experiment.

TOOLS AND MATERIALS

There's no end to the types of materials you can use for your soutache creations.

SOUTACHE (1)

Soutache is a flat braid. It comes in a wide variety of colors, and it is available in widths from 3/32" to 3/16" (2mm to 5mm). In this book, I use braids 1/8" (3mm) wide produced in the Czech Republic and made of 100 percent viscose (also called rayon). It is shiny, soft and easy to work with.

From the same manufacturer, I use a soutache braid that is made from 39 percent viscose and 61 percent acetate. It has a glossy surface, but it is stiffer than the 100 percent viscose soutache braid.

I also use polyester soutache produced in the United States. It has more of a matte look but has the same texture as the viscose/acetate braid.

Metallic soutache is made of a combination of polyester, rayon, lurex and other materials. This combination may make the soutache a little narrower and stiffer than nonmetallic soutache. It can fall apart easily, so be careful when threading a needle with this cord. The end result will be worth the extra effort.

Twisted soutache is made of rayon and polypropylene. It is soft and has a nice, silky shine. It falls apart easily, however, so tape the ends before using it. Twisted braid is available in many different sizes, but for making soutache jewelry, the perfect braid is 1/32" or 1/8" (1mm or 3mm) wide.

BEADS (2)

I use a wide variety of beads, including table-cut beads, fire-polished beads, pressed beads, shell or metallic beads, as well as round, coin, oval, drop and rectangle shapes, bicones and crystal beads. The beads I use range in size from as small as 2mm to as large as 24mm–30mm.

I also use seed beads from size 15/0 to size 8/0. Seed beads come in a variety of colors and shapes, including bugle beads, triangles, tila and hexagon-cut beads.

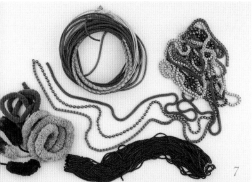

CABOCHONS AND BUTTONS (3)

Cabochons have a flat back and a domed surface and can be round, oval, rectangular, square or irregular in shape.

I also use buttons with flat backs. If you have a button that has a shank, simply cut off the shank. If the shank can't be removed (for example, on a glass button), just cut a small hole in the center of the beading foundation and glue the button to the foundation.

CRYSTALS (4)

There are tons of gorgeous crystals available, including rivolis, non-hotfix flat-back crystals, fancy stones and pendants in many shapes and sizes.

RHINESTONE CHAIN (5)

Rhinestone chain comes in several platings and sizes in a wide variety of colors. For making soutache jewelry, select smaller sizes of rhinestone chain. I use 2.1mm, 2.5mm and 3mm size chains.

FINDINGS (6)

A number of findings are used in the projects presented in this book. You will need ear wires and ear studs, metal blanks for rings, bead caps, brooches, lace terminators, jump rings and closed rings.

OTHER MATERIALS (7)

I use braided leather and round leather cords in sizes $3/32$" and $1/8$" (2mm and 3mm), different kinds of metallic chains, fringe and pompom trim to make my pieces of jewelry unique.

BEADING FOUNDATION (8)

Lacy's Stiff Stuff is one of the best innovations in modern beadwork. It comes in 8½" × 11" (21.6cm × 27.9cm) sheets and is available in nearly every bead store. It is a perfect foundation for soutache jewelry.

ULTRASUEDE OR LEATHER (9)

Use ultrasuede or leather to back your finished pieces. I usually use black leather (0.5mm–0.7mm thick), but ultrasuede can be a perfect choice for backing, too. It comes in beautiful colors and is lightweight and soft.

THREAD (10)

I use nylon thread for soutache embroidery. It is very important to match the thread to the soutache braid, so keep several

11

colors on hand, especially the basic colors of white, black, gray, brown, red, blue and green.

I also use invisible thread. It is strong and perfect for adding embellishments or for other applications in this technique.

ADHESIVE (11)

Select a strong, heavy-duty glue that's suitable for metallic and glass beads, stones and fabrics. Choose one that is flexible when it dries, rather than hard, so you can push a needle through it. I use E-6000; this glue is perfect for soutache embroidery. Use a needle or pin to apply it in small amounts for jewelry applications.

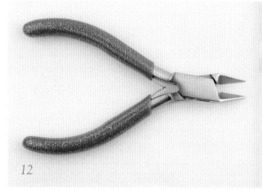

12

WIRE CUTTERS (12)

Wire cutters are excellent for cutting regular and rhinestone chains. The blades do wear down after extended use, so make sure you replace them occasionally.

PLIERS (13)

Use round-nose pliers to bend loops and pull needles through resistant points. The tapered tips allow you make loops of various sizes.

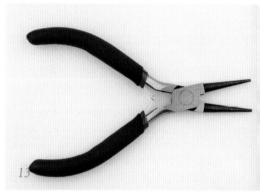

13

NEEDLES (14)

Beading needles are available in many sizes, ranging from size 10 to 15 (the larger the number, the thinner the needle). The needles fall into two types: long and short. Short beading needles are more suited to embroidery. I normally use size 10 and 12 needles. Sometimes, if I'm working with snake or box chains or tiny 15/0 seed beads, I use size 15 beading needles. They are very thin and bend easily.

OTHER HANDY TOOLS

A **standard tape measure** is useful for measuring braid, fabric and other things.

A good quality pair of **embroidery scissors** with fine, sharp points is essential for soutache embroidery.

When working with beads, it is always a good idea to have a soft surface on which to spread out your beads. I use **bead mats**, which most bead stores carry.

Good lighting is very important when you are embroidering. There are all sorts of different styles of **beading lamps** available, so you can find the perfect one for you.

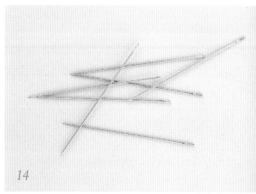

14

15

BASIC TECHNIQUES

You can find everything here that you'll need to complete the projects presented in this book. These steps will teach you how to work with soutache, and as you work through the projects using these basic instructions, you will master the techniques.

attaching beading foundation

THERE ARE TWO DIFFERENT WAYS to attach the beading foundation. Select the method to use based on the type of stone you've chosen.

FLAT BEAD OR FLAT CABOCHON

1 Apply a thin coat of glue to the back of the bead. A wooden toothpick can be very useful for spreading the glue.

2 Place the glued bead onto the beading foundation (Lacy's Stiff Stuff) and let dry completely.

3 Cut the foundation next to your bead.

4 You don't need to leave an edge, but you do need to make sure that the foundation isn't too small. The bead and the foundation must be roughly the same size.

RIVOLI OR POINTED-BACK STONE

1 Place the stone onto the beading foundation (Lacy's Stiff Stuff) and trace around it. In this case, leave a little edge all around the stone. If your stone has a nonpointed back side, trace around this side.

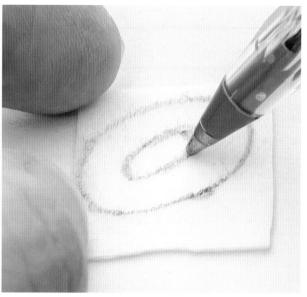

2 Draw a smaller version of the original shape in the center.

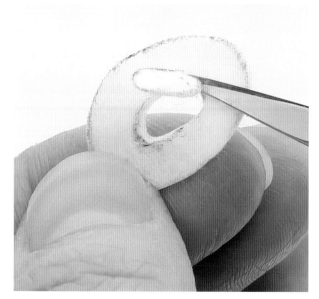

3 Cut out the shapes (at the center, start small and cut bigger if needed). You want the hole to accommodate the point on the back of the stone.

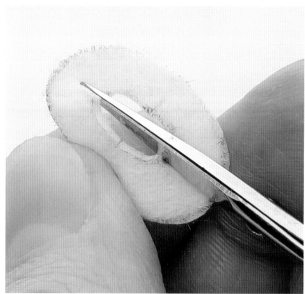

4 Cut four small slits from the middle toward each of the four sides.

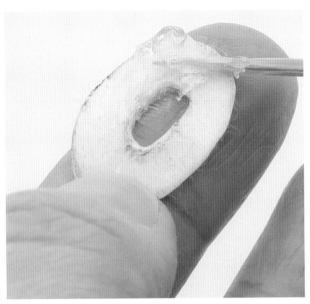

5 Apply a thin coat of glue to the beading foundation and place the stone onto the glued foundation. Let dry completely.

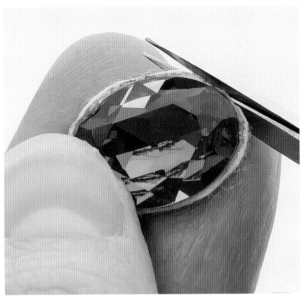

6 Cut the foundation next to your stone.

7 Now your non-flatback stone can be treated like a flat cabochon.

attaching soutache around components

THERE ARE TWO BASIC WAYS to attach soutache braids around your components: open wrapping and closed wrapping. An **open wrap** is when you use two soutache braids to wrap the bead. This can be done with a bead either with or without a foundation (when there's no foundation, the resulting piece is called a band or a soutache chain). A **closed wrap** is when you wrap only one piece of braid completely around the bead. Again, a closed wrap can be done on a bead with or without a foundation.

TIP
When you're just learning to work with soutache, apply one row of soutache braid at a time.

OPEN WRAP WITH BEAD FOUNDATION

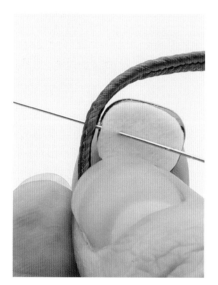  

1 After you've applied the beading foundation, thread your needle, cut the thread to a comfortable length and tie a knot at one end. Cut the soutache braids to the length specified in the instructions.

Align one piece of braid with the bead on one side, leaving a tail roughly 2" (5cm) long or the length given in the project. Insert the needle into the foundation and sew through the groove of the soutache braid.

2 Stitch down approximately ⅛" (3mm) from the previous spot and go back through the braid and the foundation.

3 Work down one side of the bead, stitching the soutache in the same way. Always place your stitches in the groove of the soutache and make sure your needle enters the beading foundation at a slight angle.

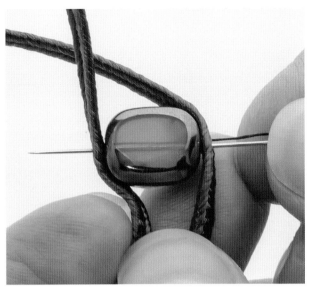

4 Once you have reached the top of the bead with the first braid, align the second braid on the other side of the bead, again leaving a 2" (5cm) tail. Start stitching the soutache in the same way.

If your bead has a hole, pass the needle through the braids and the hole, too. It helps to secure the braids and the bead together in a stronger way.

5 When you have reached the top of the bead on both sides, sew the two braids together at their meeting point. Make several stitches to secure them together.

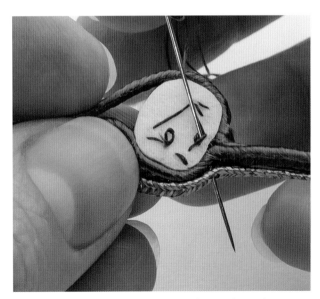

6 Add one or more additional rows of soutache in the same way, if desired. If the soutache has a woven pattern, make sure that both of your pieces are facing the same way.

7 Once you have reached the bottom of the bead, sew all braids together at their meeting point. Make several stitches to fix them together.

OPEN WRAP WITHOUT BEAD FOUNDATION

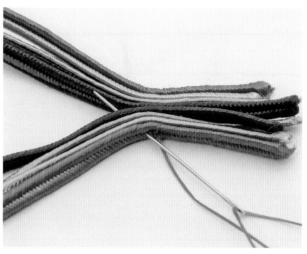

1   Thread your needle, cut the thread to a comfortable length and tie a knot at one end. Cut the soutache braids. Sew all the braids together at one point with several stitches; make sure the knot is between the braids (see page 16, step 1 for how to do this).

2   Divide the braids into two groups. Pass the needle back through one group to the center.

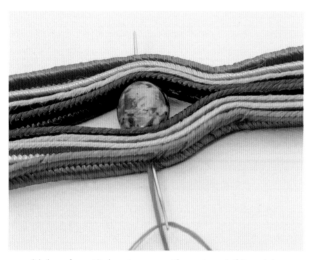

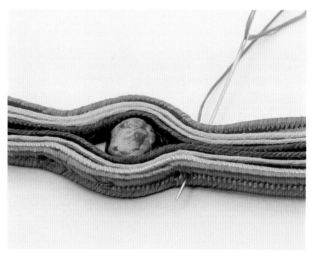

3   Make a few stitches to secure the group at this point. Thread the needle back to the center, pick up a bead and go through the other group to the outside of the soutache. The number of stitches you take depends on the size of the bead. Try to determine how much space you'll need for your bead, but don't forget to leave a little space between the bead and the two meeting points of the soutache groups.

    The bead has been fixed between the braids. Make several stitches through the braids and the bead to really secure it.

4   "Lead" the needle down one group of braids to a point below the bead by making small stitches. Stop at a point that is roughly the same distance as the point where you stitched above the bead. Stitch all braids together under the bead. Repeat these steps until the band or "chain" is the desired length.

    To make a bent chain, hold the braids in a bent shape and secure the beads between them in this same way. Pay attention to the spacing between the beads and braids; it should be consistent throughout the length of your piece.

CLOSED WRAP WITH BEAD FOUNDATION

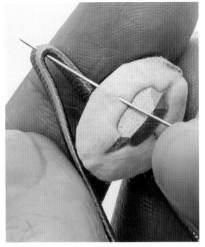

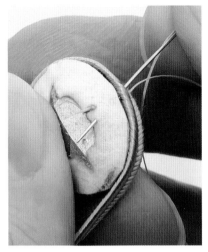

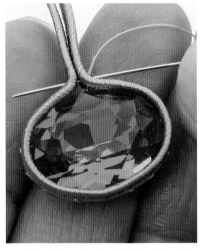

1 After you've applied the beading foundation, thread your needle, cut the thread to a comfortable length and tie a knot at one end. Cut the soutache braids to the length specified in the instructions. Align one piece of braid with the bead, insert the needle into the foundation and sew through the middle of the first braid.

2 Insert your needle back down approximately ⅛" (3mm) from the previous spot and sew through the braid and the foundation.

3 Sew the soutache to both sides of the bead in the same way. When you reach the top of the bead on both sides, sew the two ends together at their meeting point.

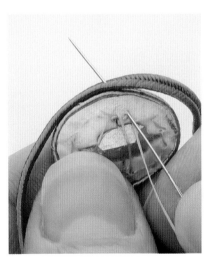

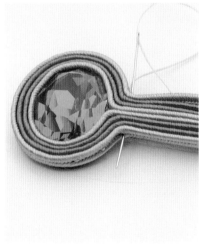

4 Add one or more additional rows of soutache in the same way, if desired.

5 Always sew the braids together at their meeting point, unless the instructions tell you differently. Make several stitches to secure them.

TIP

When you're working with closed wrapping, always start stitching in the middle of the braid unless the instructions tell you differently. It helps to keep your work the same on both sides.

CLOSED WRAP WITHOUT BEAD FOUNDATION

1 Thread your needle, cut the thread to a comfortable length and tie a knot at one end. Cut the soutache braids. You will start stitching in the middle of the braids, so cover the knot first. Insert the needle through the braid with the knot on what will be the inside of the braid. Stitch back through approximately ⅛" (3mm) from the previous stitch.

2 Add one or more additional rows of soutache to the first braid. Make sure the knot stays between the braids.

3 Fix all braids together in the middle. Secure them several times and pick up your bead.

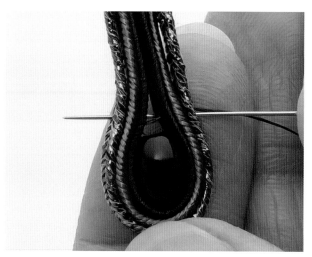

4 Wrap the braids around the bead; now you have two soutache groups. Stitch one group together at a point in line with the bottom of the bead. Make a stitch near the previous spot, sewing from the outside through to the center and through the other soutache group.

5 Finally, sew all braids together at the point under the bead with several stitches.

attaching soutache around a closed ring

THIS STEP IS ONE OF MY FAVORITE TECHNIQUES. It may look complicated, but it's a great technique to learn because the shape you'll get is beautiful, and it can be used in many ways.

1 Using invisible thread, thread the needle and tie a knot at one end. Cut the soutache braids. Align one piece of braid with the closed ring, leaving a 1" (2.5cm) tail (or as noted in the project). Sew through the braid and insert the needle to one side of the ring.

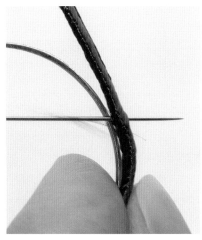

2 Pass the needle back through the braid on the other side of the closed ring.

3 Bring the needle back through the soutache roughly ⅛" (3mm) away from the first stitch. Continue stitching the braid all the way around in the same way.

4 Once you have reached the top of the ring, sew the braids together at their meeting point. Make several stitches to fix them together.

Add one or more additional rows of soutache, if desired, but work only one row at a time.

5 While stitching the second braid all the way around, don't secure it through the closed ring; simply sew the braids together.

6 After the rows of soutache have been sewn, make a few stitches to secure them at the meeting point.

stitching a row of beads

WHEN YOU PLACE THE BEADS SIDE BY SIDE, they should barely touch each other. Be prepared to make adjustments in your work so the beads aren't too crowded. If the beads are too close together, they will create an uneven and wavy surface.

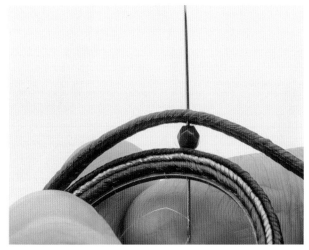

1 Poke your needle through the base of the braids, pick up a bead and stitch into a new braid. Work with only one new braid at a time.

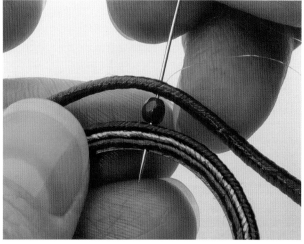

2 Stitch back through the braid and the bead and bring the needle out the back of the work.

3 Keep adding more beads in the same way until you have as many as you'd like in the row.

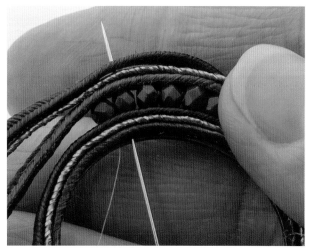

4 After the first row of soutache has been sewn, add the other pieces of soutache on top of the first, sewing them together through the beads and the base. Always bring your needle out the back of the work.

making curves

YOU'LL USE TWO BASIC METHODS TO MAKE CURVES; the first creates an open curve, the second a closed curve.

OPEN CURVE

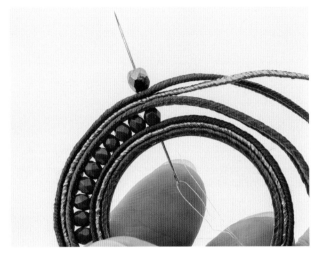

1 Bring your needle out from the base and pick up a bead.

2 Hold the braids in the shape you want to achieve and pass the needle through where the hole of the bead naturally meets the braids.

3 Sew back through the braids and the bead. Bring the needle out the back of the work.

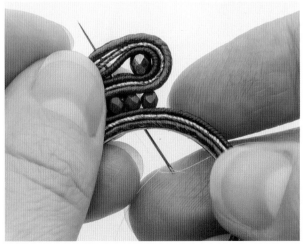

4 Lead the needle slightly away through the base of the braids and sew the upper pieces of soutache (the ones folded over the bead) to the base at one point. Make a few stitches to secure. (You can stitch through only the top layer of the base, if you prefer.)

CLOSED CURVE

1 Bring your needle out from the base and pick up a bead.

2 Hold the braids in the shape you want to achieve and pass the needle through where the hole of the bead naturally meets the braids.

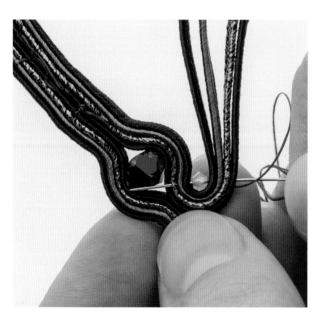

3 Sew back through the braids and the bead and bring your needle out the back of the work.

4 Sew the braids together, then secure the ends of the soutache to the back of the work using several stitches. Apply a small amount of glue to the spot where you want to cut the excess soutache; when the glue starts to dry, cut off the excess soutache.

attaching rhinestone chain

ATTACHING A RHINESTONE CHAIN requires patience and care. A little practice helps in the process, and using invisible thread will help keep your stitches light. In this section, you will learn to attach the chain between braids and on top of braids.

BETWEEN BRAIDS

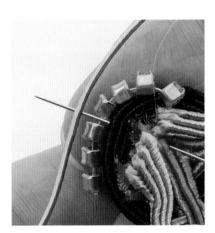

1 Using invisible thread, bring the needle up from the base. At almost the same point, take the needle down, but do not pull the thread completely. This creates a loop of thread.

2 Pass one rhinestone through the loop and tighten the thread securely over the chain. When you're applying the rhinestone chain to the bottom of your work, start attaching the chain in the middle to ensure there's enough chain and braid for both sides.

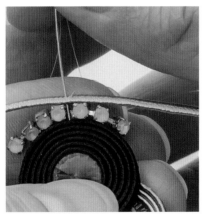

3 Lead the needle out to the same point, behind the rhinestone's connection, and stitch into the new braid.

4 Stitch back to the base in front of the connection. It is enough to secure every other stone by repeating these same steps.

5 Now you can add one or more rows of soutache. Simply sew them to the first braid; there's no need to fix them through the rhinestone chain and the base of the braids.

1 With invisible thread, make a loop for the first rhinestone. Bring the needle up from the base. At almost the same point, take the needle back without tightening the thread.

2 Pull the first rhinestone through the loop and tighten the thread completely over the connection between the first two rhinestones in the chain.

3 Lead the needle out to the same point and stitch over the connection.

4 Fix the chain around the base as instructed in the project. Sew back up at the next connection and continue stitching the chain in the same way.

making a hand-embroidered clasp

THIS CLASP WILL HOLD YOUR JEWELRY CLOSED, so as you're working, make sure the two parts fit snugly. Also, don't forget to keep your stitches hidden. As your technique improves, this will become an easy step in the process.

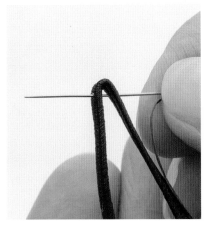

1 Thread your needle, cut the thread to a comfortable length and tie a knot at one end. Cut the soutache braids. Fold the first braid in half and sew the sides together at one point.

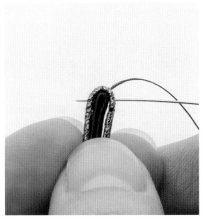

2 Place a second braid over the first and secure with a stitch.

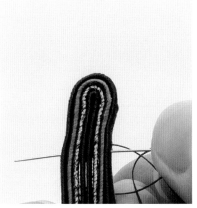

3 Add the remaining braids in the same way. Lead the needle ⅝" (1.5cm) farther down the braids and sew them together.

4 Lead the needle to the back of the work, keeping the stitches hidden. Bring the needle through the braids to the front. Pick up a bead and place it on top of the braids. Make a few stitches to secure the bead.

5 Lead the needle another ⅝" (1.5cm) down the braids and sew the braids together. Lead the needle to the back and sew another bead on top of the braids. Leave roughly ⅜" (1cm) distance between the bottom of the first bead and the top of the second bead.

6 Divide the braids into two groups. Make a few stitches down one group of braids, pass the needle through to the center and pick up a bead.

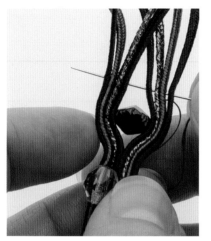

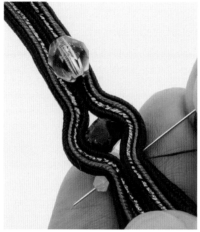

7 Go through the other group of braids to the outside; the bead is in place between the braids. Make several stitches through the braids and the bead to really secure it.

Lead the needle a few stitches past the bead on either side and secure all braids together below the bead.

8 Bring the needle out at the meeting point and pick up a bead.

9 Make a closed curve (see page 20) around the bead. Repeat on the other side.

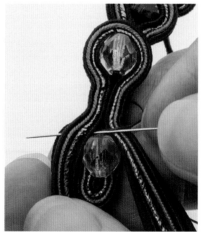

10 To make the other half of the clasp, thread your needle, cut the thread to a comfortable length and tie a knot at one end. Cut the soutache braids. Sew all the braids together in the middle, covering the knot as described on page 16, step 1.

11 Sew the braids together into one group, then bend the braids to form a loop. Measure this first loop to the upper bead of the other half of the clasp; the bead must fit snugly inside the loop. Sew the rows of braid together to secure the loop. Continue to sew the braids on one side to form a second loop; check that the second bead will fit inside this loop.

12 To finish this half of the clasp, repeat steps 6-9.

Place the curves of each clasp atop one end of the necklace or bracelet. Stitch the clasps to the jewelry, sewing through the layers of soutache. Use several stitches to secure them, cut off the braid ends if necessary and apply glue to the ends. The leather used to finish the jewelry (page 29) will help secure the clasps, as well.

attaching soutache and beads above a base

DON'T PULL YOUR STITCHES TOO TIGHT for this technique because this will create bumps or waves in your work. Keep the braids loose above the base, but also secure them several times to the back of the work.

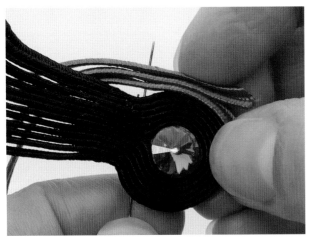

1. Using invisible thread, thread your needle, cut the thread to a comfortable length and tie a knot at one end. Cut the soutache braids. Bring your needle out of the base at the meeting point. Insert the needle through the braids being added, leaving a tail 1" (2.5cm) long or the length given in the project.

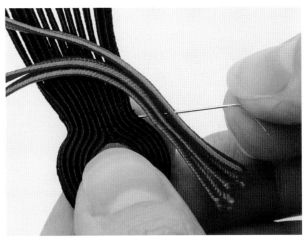

2. Pass the needle back through the braids being added and bring the needle out on the other side of the meeting point.

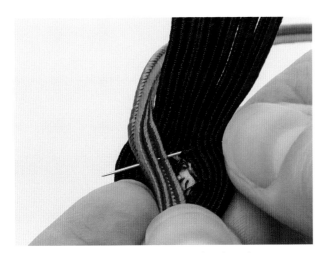

3. Insert the needle back through the braids and come out the back center of the work. By inserting the needle at an angle, you will pass through several of the base braids for a more secure attachment. Pass the needle through the braids being added.

4. Pass the needle back through the base at the same spot.

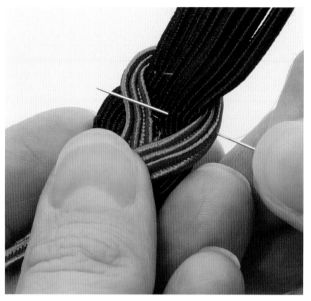

5 Wrap the group of braids around the base and stitch them together.

6 To finish, secure the braids to the side of the base, then sew the braids together at the back of the work.

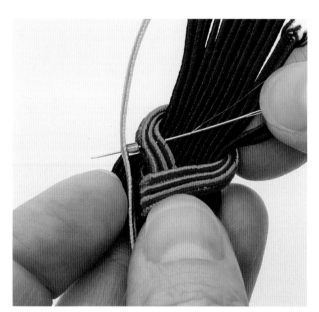

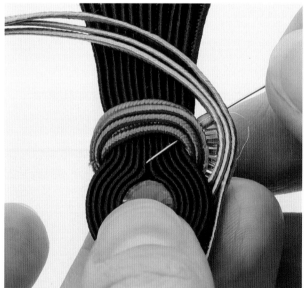

7 Slide your needle through on one side, pick up a bead and go through a new braid, leaving a tail 1" (2.5cm) long or the length given in the project. Stitch back through the bead and the braid. Pass the needle through the same spot and through the bead and braid.

8 Add two (or the number of pieces given in the project) additional pieces of soutache to the needle. In this case, don't bring the needle out of the back of the work. Simply sew the beads between the braids. Here it is easier to stitch multiple braids simultaneously, because the braids under the row of beads are loose and too many stitches might create an uneven or wavy finish.

creating shapes

INCREASE YOUR SKILLS by trying these soutache shapes. You won't need beading foundation, but it is very important to sew with small, accurate stitches. With a little practice, you'll create perfect shapes.

LEAVES

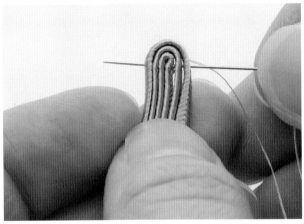

1 Thread your needle, cut the thread to a comfortable length and tie a knot at one end. Cut the soutache braids. Fold the braids in half. Sew them together about 1/16" (1mm–2mm) from the fold, covering the knot (see page 16, step 1). This will be the peak.

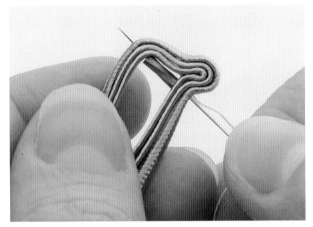

2 Separate the braids into two equal groups. Sew up through the bottom group, close to the fold, pick up a bugle bead and sew through the upper rows of soutache where the hole of the bead meets the braids. Make several stitches to secure it.

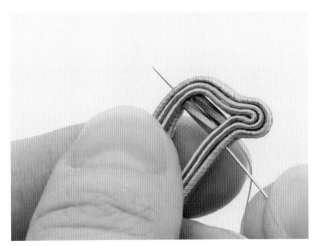

3 Lead the needle down one bead width away from the previous stitch. Sew up through the bottom group, pick up a bugle bead and sew through the upper rows of soutache where the hole of the bead meets the braids. Make several stitches to secure it.

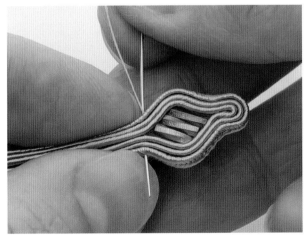

4 Sew one more bugle bead between the braids in the same way. Bring the needle out on the upper side, align the bottom rows of soutache with the upper group and secure them together with several stitches.

DIAMONDS

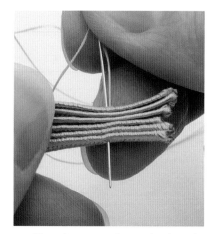

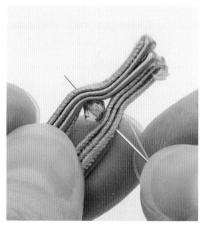

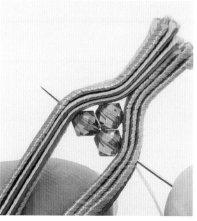

1 Thread your needle, cut the thread to a comfortable length and tie a knot at one end. Cut the soutache braids. Sew them together near one end.

2 Divide the braids into two equal groups. Sew through one group of soutache, pick up a bead and sew through the other soutache group where the hole of the bead meets the braids. Secure the bead with several stitches.

3 Lead the needle down one bead width away from the previous stitch. Pick up two beads and make a few stitches to secure them between the two soutache groups.

LONG CURVES

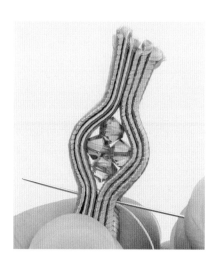

4 Sew another bead between the braids in the same way. Sew all the braids together at their meeting point with several stitches.

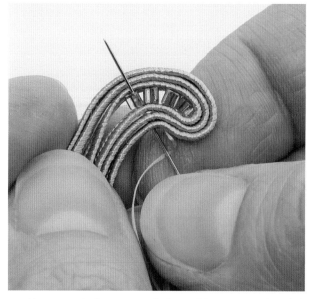

1 You can make long curves that are either open or closed at the ends. Simply hold the braids in the shape you want to achieve and sew the beads between them.

covering the back

THIS WILL ALWAYS BE THE VERY LAST STEP in the soutache jewelry-making process. Make sure your scissors are really sharp so the leather pieces are neat and tidy. Be careful not to use too much glue or your work will fall apart.

1 Place the finished work on the leather and trace around the work.

2 Cut out the shape, making the backing piece just a little larger than the work.

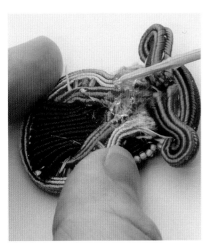

3 Apply a thin coat of glue to the middle back of the work piece and place the leather onto the glue.

4 Apply a thin coat of glue to the rest of the leather and carefully press it to the back of the work.

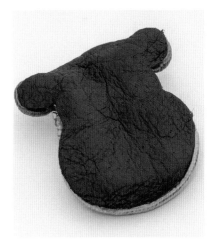

5 Continue to glue the leather to each part. Make sure the glue extends to the outer edge of the work but isn't so thick it oozes out when pressed onto the backing. Trim the leather to the size of the work.

the projects

THE PROJECTS IN THIS BOOK WILL GIVE ALL READERS—
from beginners to the more advanced—an opportunity
to put the basics of soutache embroidery into practice
while creating beautiful jewelry. Whether you choose
to make a project exactly as it appears in this book or
to incorporate an entrancing component into your own
design, these projects will guide you through a journey
of discovery.

With the Apollo Pendant, I created a design that requires you to attach soutache around a closed ring, and
the Caprice Earrings were designed to help you practice
applying a rhinestone chain. I used long fringe to add
interest to the Mexico Pendant, and the India Choker
was inspired by that beautiful country.

Once you've practiced working with soutache, challenge yourself to create your own fabulous one-of-a-
kind jewelry pieces.

ZIMA
earrings

IMAGINE YOURSELF IN A WINTER WONDERLAND, wearing these simple, feminine and refined earrings. This project is a perfect choice for beginners. I've listed the materials I used, but don't worry if you don't have exactly what's on the list. Listen to your inner voice and use elements and colors you like. Just be sure to use the same size beads that I used.

FINISHED SIZE

Approximately 1½" × 1" (3.8cm × 2.5cm)

MATERIALS

25¼" (64cm) each of soutache in three colors:

A: dark gray

B: metallic silver

C: metallic gunmetal

2 Czech flat oval beads, 14mm × 10mm (beige brown picasso)

2 coin beads, 8mm (purple marble)

2 Czech oval cathedral beads, 4mm × 6mm (hyacinth orange/picasso ends)

2 Czech fire-polished beads, 3mm (metallic copper matte)

2 Miyuki tila beads, 5mm (metallic copper matte)

26 Toho triangle beads, 2.2mm (opaque frosted rainbow iris)

2 Czech fire-polished beads, 2mm (jet)

2 ear studs (copper)

beading foundation (Lacy's Stiff Stuff)

leather or ultrasuede for backing

thread

embroidery needle

tape measure

scissors

glue

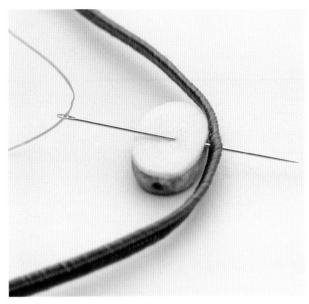

1 Glue the Czech oval beads and the coin beads to the beading foundation. When dry, cut around the beads. Cut a 6¼" (16cm) braid of each color. With a flat oval bead and braid A, make a closed wrap (page 15).

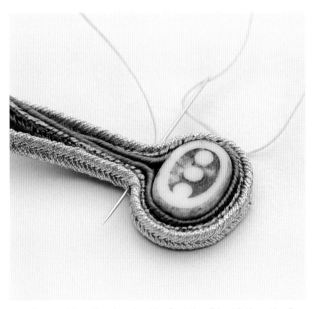

2 Sew on the other two braids, first the C braid, then the B braid, and fix them together at the meeting point. Make a few stitches to secure them.

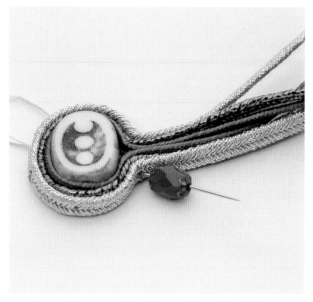

3 Sew out from one side of the meeting point, pick up an oval cathedral bead and make a closed curve (page 20) around it. This is curve 1. When you're working on the second earring, be sure that this curve is on the opposite side of the meeting point.

4 Sew out from the other side of the meeting point, pick up a 3mm fire-polished bead and make a closed curve. This is curve 2.

5 Fix a tila bead on top of the meeting point. Sew through both holes of the bead two times.

6 Cut a 6¼" (16cm) braid of each color. Pass the needle through the bottom of curve 2 from the back of the piece. Pass the needle through a triangle bead and then through the three braids in this order: B, C, A. Continue to sew a row of beads to this curve (page 18).

7 Sew a total of thirteen triangle beads to the curve. Fix the upper braids to the curve 1 braids at one point. Sew up through this point and pick up a coin bead. Make a closed curve, stitching through the beading foundation. Pass the needle through the hole of the bead, too.

8 Fix a 2mm fire-polished bead to the bottom of the coin bead where the triangle bead braids are sewn to the braids of curve 1. Lead all braids to the back of the piece, cut off the extra braids and apply glue to the braid ends. Tie off the thread with several knots, and clip the thread close.

9 Place the piece on the leather, trace around the piece and cut out the shape. Use a needle to pierce a hole in the backing (behind the coin bead part). From the wrong side of the leather, pass the ear stud through the hole. Apply a thin coat of glue to secure.

10 Cover the back of the work (page 29). Repeat all the steps to make a second earring, but mirror the orientation and placement of the beads.

ADEL *pendant*

SIMPLE, BUT ISN'T IT BEAUTIFUL? I love the luscious colors and the unique clasp. Upon receiving the ball chain, I realized that I had the perfect match for this pendant.

FINISHED SIZE

Approximately 22" (56cm) long; pendant, excluding drop, is approximately 1½" × 1¼" (3.8cm × 3.2cm)

MATERIALS

soutache braids in three colors:

  A: cream, 19¾" (50cm)

  B: cream gold, 41¼" (105cm)

  C: golden brown, 29½" (75cm)

3 Czech glass square beads, 10mm (opal orange)

Czech fire-polished beads, 3mm, in 2 colors:

  A: opaque lime green, 3 beads

  B: light blue picasso, 8 beads

1 Czech druk round bead, 6mm (sage green)

3 Miyuki tila beads, 5mm (matte opaque mustard)

1 Czech glass teardrop bead, 16mm × 12mm (olive green)

75 seed beads, 15/0 (buttermilk)

1 basket bead cap, 5mm (antique copper)

16½" (42cm) ball chain, 3.2mm (bronze tone)

1 magnetic clasp

2 jump rings, 5mm (bronze tone)

beading foundation (Lacy's Stiff Stuff)

leather or ultrasuede for backing

thread and invisible thread

embroidery needle

tape measure

scissors

glue

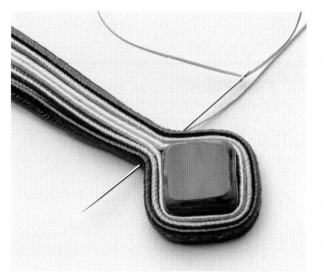

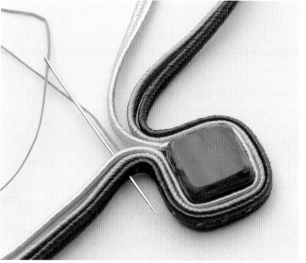

1 Glue the square beads to the beading foundation. When dry, cut around the beads.

Cut a 7" (18cm) braid of each color. Thread the needle. Using the A braid, make a closed wrap (page 15) around one square bead. Sew on the other two braids, B first and then C, and fix them together at the meeting point. Make a few stitches to secure them.

2 Divide the braids into two groups of three braids each. Take a few stitches to lead the needle approximately ³⁄₈" (1cm) away from the meeting point on either side.

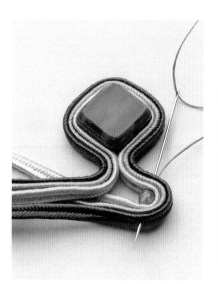

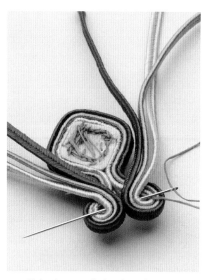

3 Insert the needle back through the braids, pick up a B-colored fire-polished bead, bend the braids over the bead and pass the needle through the braids.

4 Place the braids behind the bead and fix the curve with several stitches.

5 Take the needle back to the meeting point and create another curve on the other side, following steps 2-4.

Sew the two curves together several times at the back of the base. Then tie off the thread with several knots and clip the thread close. Don't cut the braids yet.

6 Thread your needle and cut the thread to a comfortable length. Cut two 6" (15cm) B braids and one 6" (15cm) C braid. Pass the needle out from the base on one side, roughly in line with the corner of the square bead. Pick up two 15/0 seed beads and pass the needle through a B braid, leaving a tail of approximately ³⁄₈" (1cm).

7 Sew approximately 33 double rows of 15/0 seed beads around the base (page 18). Sew on the second B braid and the C braid. Adjust the braids as you take each stitch. When stitching the braids, never pull the thread tight because doing so can make the braids wavy.

8 Cut off the braid ends and apply glue to the ends. Tie off the thread with several knots and clip close.

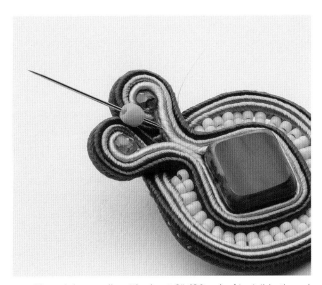

9 Thread the needle with about 8" (20cm) of invisible thread and tie a knot at one end. Referring to the photo, pass the needle up through the braids, to one side of the meeting point, and fix an A-colored fire-polished bead to this point with several stitches.

10 Sew a 6mm druk round bead on top of the braids, above the square bead. Use several stitches to secure it. Tie off the thread with several knots and clip close.

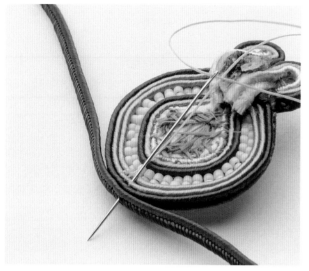

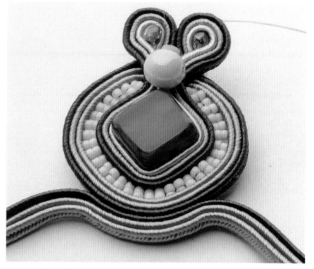

11 Thread the needle. Cut two 4¾" (12cm) B braids and one 4¾" (12cm) C braid. Sew out of the bottom of the base, in the center, and pass the needle through the center of the C braid.

12 Sew the C braid ⅜" (1cm) to the left and to the right of the center point. Sew on the other two B braids, too.

13 Referring to the photo, bring the needle out from the base and pick up a B-colored fire-polished bead.

14 Make a closed curve (page 20) around the bead. Repeat on the other side, then cut off the braids and apply glue to the ends. Tie off the thread with several knots and clip close.

Thread the needle with invisible thread. Pass the needle up through the braids under the row of seed beads roughly ⅛" (3.2mm) from the center. Sew a tila bead on top of the braids with several stitches.

15 Sew a tila bead to each side of the first. Lead the needle out through the braids at the center. Fix a seed bead, a basket bead cap and a teardrop bead to the bottom, securing them with several stitches. Tie off the thread.

16 Thread the needle and cut the thread to a comfortable length. Cut a 6" (15cm) braid of each color. Make a closed wrap around a square bead using the braids in this order: A, B, C. Sew the braids together at the meeting point with several stitches.

17 Sew out from the meeting point, pick up a B-colored fire-polished bead and make a closed curve around it.

18 Make a closed curve around a B-colored bead on the other side. Cut off the braids and apply glue to the ends. Tie off the thread with several knots and clip close.

Thread the needle with invisible thread. Sew an A-colored fire-polished bead on top of the meeting point. Refer to the photo and sew three 15/0 seed beads and a jump ring between the two curves.

19 Repeat steps 16–18 using the third square bead. Add half of the magnetic clasp to each jump ring.

Apply a small amount of glue to the back side, between the curve's braids. Place one end of the chain in the glue and let it dry. Sew through one side of the curve's braids, wrap the thread around the section between the last two balls in the chain two times, and pass the needle through the other side of the curve's braids.

Repeat with the other end of the chain and the other square component.

20 Find the center of the long piece of chain. Use the glue-and-sew process described in step 19 to attach the center of the chain to the back of the pendant.

21 Cover the back of the work with leather (page 29) to finish the pendant.

BAROQUE
bracelet

BAROQUE ART IS CHARACTERIZED BY GREAT DRAMA, rich, deep color, intense light and dark shadows. The mixture of claret and bright lime in this bracelet is a feast for your eyes and will take you back to the seventeenth century.

FINISHED SIZE
Approximately 7½" (19cm)

MATERIALS

soutache braids in two colors:

A: claret, 84½" (215cm)

B: metallic bronze, 33½" (85cm)

1 vintage glass oval cabochon, 18mm (red brown)

8 Czech glass round antique-cut faceted beads, 9mm (opaque lime picasso)

1 Miyuki tila bead, 5mm (matte metallic copper)

Czech fire-polished beads, 3mm, in two colors:

A: matte metallic copper, 7 beads

B: opaque green, 6 beads

30 Miyuki delica beads, 11/0 (antique copper)

2 Czech glass fluted cathedral beads, 9mm (red picasso)

beading foundation (Lacy's Stiff Stuff)

leather or ultrasuede for backing

thread and invisible thread

embroidery needle

tape measure

scissors

glue

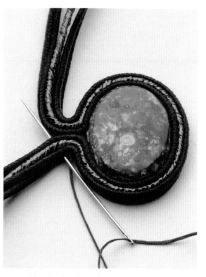

1 Glue the vintage glass oval cabochon on the beading foundation. When dry, cut around the bead.

Cut two 8" (20cm) A braids and one 8" (20cm) B braid. Thread the needle and make a closed wrap (page 15) around the cabochon with one A braid.

2 Sew on the other two braids, B first, then A, and fix them together at the meeting point. Make a few stitches to secure them.

3 Divide the braids into two groups of three braids each. Take stitches along one group to lead the needle to roughly ⅜" (1cm) from the meeting point.

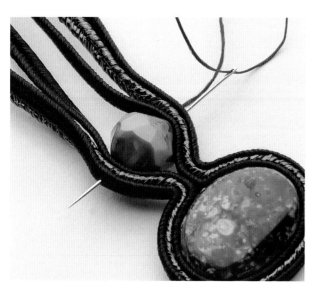

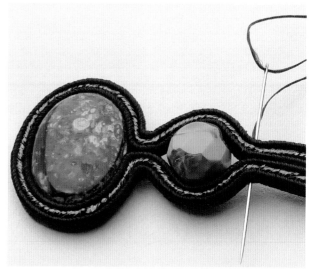

4 Pick up a round faceted bead and pass the needle through the other soutache group. Secure the bead between the braids with several stitches.

5 Lead the needle up through one soutache group to roughly ⅜" (1cm) down the braid and sew the two soutache groups together below the bead.

6 Repeating steps 4–5, fix two more round faceted beads between the braids. Set aside this element.

7 Cut four 4" (10cm) braids from color A and two 4" (10cm) braids from color B. Thread your needle, cut the thread to about 13¾" (35cm) and tie a knot at one end. Place the braids in this order: A, B, A, A, B, A. With the ends all lined up and the braids facing the same way, sew the braids together at one point about ¾" (2cm) from the end.

8 Divide the braids into two groups of three braids. Lead the needle ⅜" (1cm) away from the meeting point through one set of braids. Pick up a round faceted bead and pass the needle through the other soutache group. Secure the bead between the braids with several stitches.

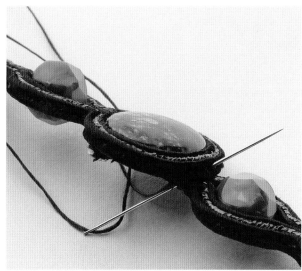

9 Lead the needle ⅜" (1cm) down one group of braids and sew the two soutache groups together below the bead. Add two more beads in the same way.

10 Sew this element to the middle back of the base cabochon and through the braids. Fix them together with several stitches. Cut off the remaining braids and place glue on the ends.

11 Pass the needle up through the braids between the cabochon and the first bead on that element. Sew a tila bead on top of the braids at that point. Tie off the thread with several knots and clip the thread close.

12 Thread your needle with invisible thread. Pass the needle through the back of the cabochon, roughly ¼" (6.4mm) away from the center of the side, and pick up three A-colored fire-polished beads.

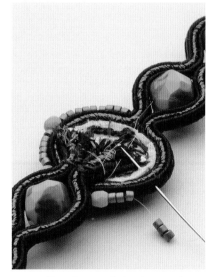

13 Pass the needle down into the base next to where the third bead rests, pulling the thread and beads down tight.

Pass the needle back up from the underside to where the first bead was strung. Pass through the three beads and pick up a B-colored fire-polished bead.

14 Pass the needle back down into the base. Bring the needle back up between the last A bead and the B bead. Go through the B bead and pick up three 11/0 delica beads. Pass the needle down into the base next to where the third delica bead rests, pulling the thread and beads down tightly.

15 Pass the needle back up again between the last two delica beads and pick up three more 11/0 delica beads. Take the needle back down into the base.

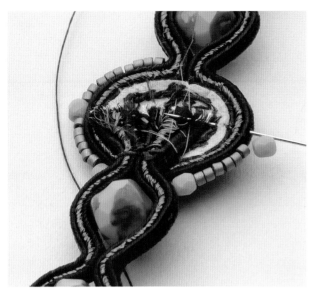

16 Come back up between the last two delicas, go through the last delica bead and pick up a B-colored bead. Pass the needle down into the base next to the B bead.

17 Following the previous steps, sew nine 11/0 delica beads to the cabochon, stitching down into the base every three beads. Repeat steps 14–17 on the other side of the cabochon.

18 Cut three 8¾" (22cm) braids of color A and one 8¾" (22cm) braid of color B for one half of the clasp. Cut the same braids for the second half of the clasp. Align and stack the braids for both halves in this order: A, A, B, A. Make a hand-embroidered clasp (page 23) using two round antique-cut faceted beads on top of the braids, one fluted cathedral bead between the braids, two A-colored fire-polished beads for the curves and one B-colored fire-polished bead on the top of the meeting points.

19 Sew the clasps to the base and cover the back of the work (page 29).

ANGELINE
necklace

THIS ELEGANT NECKLACE is delicate yet bold, like the Indian summer. I chose a beautiful salmon picasso bead and paired it with delightful turquoise, brown and golden beige braids. Simply beautiful.

FINISHED SIZE
Approximately 19¼" (49cm) long, including drop

MATERIALS
soutache braids in three colors:

    A: light brown, 2½ yards (230cm)

    B: golden beige, 4¼ yards (390cm)

    C: turquoise, 1¾ yards (160cm)

1 Czech oval bead, 17mm × 13mm (salmon picasso)

22 Toho hybrid triangle beads, 3mm (frosted apollo)

Czech fire-polished beads, 3mm, in two colors:

    A: metallic copper, 10 beads

    B: light turquoise, 6 beads

2 Czech oval beads, 14mm × 10mm (milky picasso blue caramel)

4 Czech leaf beads, 12mm (orange picasso)

2 Czech druk round beads, 3mm (opaque goldenrod)

6 Miyuki twisted bugle beads, 6mm (matte metallic patina iris)

1 Miyuki delica bead, 11/0 (matte metallic copper)

1 Swarovski teardrop pendant, 16mm (crystal copper)

16 Czech glass round beads, 6mm (opaque orange and olive picasso)

2 Czech fire-polished beads, 8mm (transparent peach)

1 basket bead cap, 5mm (antique copper)

beading foundation (Lacy's Stiff Stuff)

leather or ultrasuede for backing

thread and invisible thread

embroidery needle

tape measure

scissors

glue

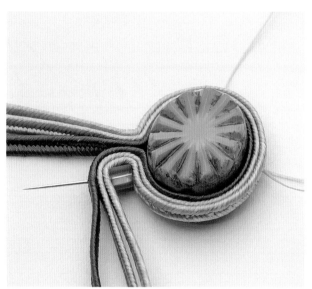

1 Glue all three oval beads and the leaf beads on the beading foundation. When dry, cut around the beads. Cut two 6¼" (16cm) B braids and one 6¼" (16cm) A braid.

Thread the needle and make a closed wrap (page 15) using the 17mm × 13mm oval bead and the A braid. Sew on the two B braids and fix them together at their meeting point. Make a few stitches to secure them.

2 Divide the braids into two groups of three. Pass the needle up through the braids of the base roughly ⅛" (3.2mm) from the meeting point. Pick up a triangle bead and bend three of the braids over the bead. Pass the needle up through the braids, then stitch back through the braids and the bead farther down the base.

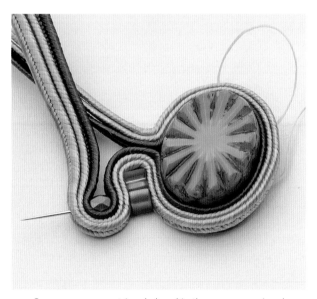

3 Sew on one more triangle bead in the same way. Lead the needle through this outer bead to the outer edge of the piece. Pick up an A-colored fire-polished bead and make a closed curve (page 20) around it.

4 Repeat steps 2–3 on the other side, then tie off the thread with several knots and clip the thread close. Set this element aside.

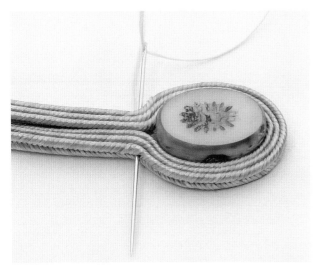

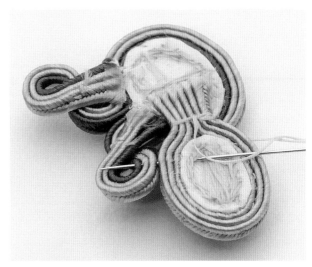

5 Thread the needle, cut the thread to a comfortable length and tie a knot at one end. Cut three 4¼" (11cm) B braids and make a closed wrap around one of the 14mm × 10mm oval beads. Sew the braids together at the meeting point with several stitches.

Repeat this step using the other 14mm × 10mm oval bead and three more B braids.

6 Cut off the remaining braids and apply glue to the braid ends of both elements. Tie off the threads and clip close.

Sew these elements to the back of the larger element. Place the smaller elements as shown in the photo. Sew them to the back of the base and to the curves around the A beads.

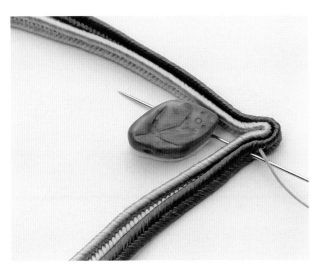

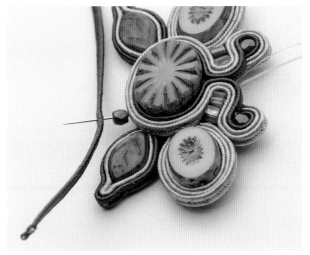

7 Thread the needle and cut a 4" (10cm) braid of colors A and C. Fold the braids in half with the C braid on the inside. Sew them together ¹⁄₁₆" (1mm–2mm) from the fold, covering the knot (page 16, step 1). This will be the peak. Make a stitch down one side of the peak and add one leaf bead. Make a closed wrap around the bead.

Repeat this step with the second leaf bead and two more A and C braids. Cut off the remaining braids and apply glue to the braid ends of both elements.

8 Sew the two leaves to the back of the base on either side of the larger oval bead. Fix them to the base and to the sides of the smaller oval beads, too.

Cut two 4¼" (11cm) B braids and one 4¼" (11cm) A braid. Pass the needle through the braids at the bottom of the work, next to the leaf bead element on either side. Pick up an A-colored fire-polished bead. Stitch into the A braid, leaving a 1¼" (3cm) tail.

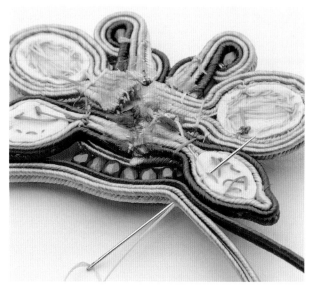

9 Stitch a row of beads (page 18) using six A-colored beads and the braids in the order A, B, B.

When the beads and the braids have been sewn, fix the separate braids to the sides of the leaf elements. Use several stitches to secure them.

10 Pass the needle out from the previous point and pick up a B-colored fire-polished bead.

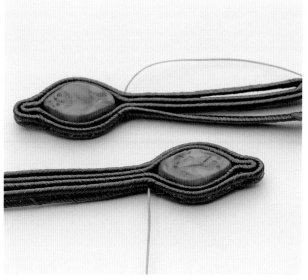

11 Make a closed curve. Repeat on the other side. Cut off the remaining braids, apply a thin coat of glue to the ends, tie off the thread with several knots and clip close.

12 Thread the needle and cut four 4" (10cm) braids of color A. Fold two of the braids in half. Sew them together 1/16" (1mm–2mm) from the fold, covering the knot. This will be the peak. Make a stitch down one side of the peak and add one leaf bead. Make a closed wrap around the bead. Repeat with the remaining braids and leaf bead.

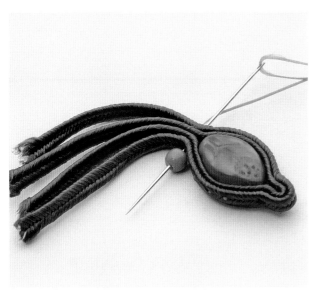

13 Sew out from the leaf meeting point on one of the leaf elements and pick up a druk round bead.

14 Make a closed curve around the druk bead. Repeat with the second druk bead on the other leaf element, but make the curve on the opposite side of the meeting point, as shown.

15 Cut two 7" (18cm) braids of color B. Make a soutache leaf shape (page 27) with three bugle beads. Make a second leaf shape with two more lengths of B braid and three more bugle beads. Sew these elements around the leaf bead elements as shown. Cut off the remaining braids, apply a thin coat of glue to the braid ends, tie off the thread with several knots and clip close.

16 Thread the needle with invisible thread and bring the needle out from the bottom center of the base of the oval bead element. Pick up the 11/0 delica bead, the basket bead cap and the teardrop pendant. Thread the needle back through the bead cap and delica bead, then secure them to the base with several stitches.

17 Referring to the photo, fix one leaf element to the braids around one 14mm × 10mm oval using an A-colored fire-polished bead and a triangle bead. Attach the second leaf element to the other oval bead in the same way. Secure with several stitches. Tie off the thread with several knots and clip close.

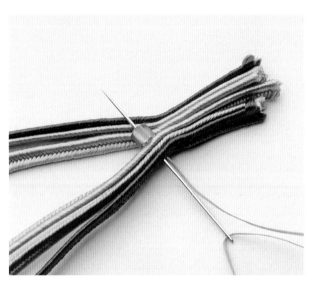

18 Thread your needle, cut the thread to a longer length and tie a knot at one end. Cut two 10" (25cm) braids of each color. Place the braids in the following order: A, B, C, C, B, A. Sew the six pieces of soutache together at one point and cover the knot. Divide the braids into two groups of three and fix one triangle bead between the braids.

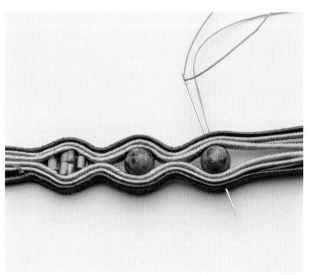

19 Fix three more triangle beads between the braids to form a soutache diamond shape (page 28). Sew the braids together after the last triangle bead.

Next stitch eight 6mm glass round beads between the braids using the open wrap technique (page 14). You are making half of the chain of the necklace, so you want this piece to be a little curved. Just hold the braids in a gentle curve and sew the beads between them. Repeat steps 17–18 to make the other half of the chain, curving the braids in the opposite direction.

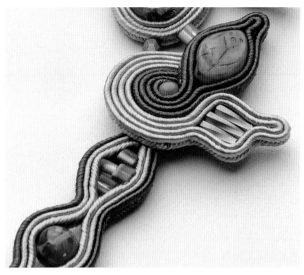

20 Cut two 8" (20cm) braids of color B and one 8" (20cm) braid of colors A and C for one half of the clasp. Cut the same braids for the other half of the clasp. Align and stack the braids in this order for both halves: A, C, B, B. Make a hand-embroidered clasp (pages 23–24), using the two 8mm fire-polished beads on top of the braids, four triangle beads between the braids in a diamond shape and two B-colored beads for the curves.

21 Sew the diamond end of one chain to the leaf element of the base. Sew them together with several stitches. Repeat on the other side.

22 Sew the other end of each chain to one half of the clasp. Cover the back of the work (page 29). Cover the back of the clasps, too.

SOPHIA
earrings

I REALLY ENJOYED creating these Italian-style earrings. The colors and the beautiful metal rose beads give them a real dolce vita feeling.

MATERIALS

soutache braids in three colors:

    A: white cream, 33½" (85cm)

    B: light silver gray, 22" (56cm)

    C: metallic copper, 11" (28cm)

2 Swarovski mini oval beads, 10mm × 8mm (crystal rose gold)

4 Swarovski bicone beads, 4mm (crystal chili pepper)

2 metal rose beads, 7.5mm (matte yellow gold)

2 seed beads, 15/0 (gold)

2 Swarovski teardrop pendants, 16mm (crystal rose patina)

2 Swarovski mini square beads, 8mm (tangerine)

Swarovski bicone beads, 3mm, in two colors:

    A: tangerine, 4 beads

    B: crystal rose gold, 4 beads

2 basket bead caps, 6mm (antique copper)

2 ear wires with flower (copper)

beading foundation (Lacy's Stiff Stuff)

leather or ultrasuede for backing

thread and invisible thread

embroidery needle

tape measure

scissors

glue

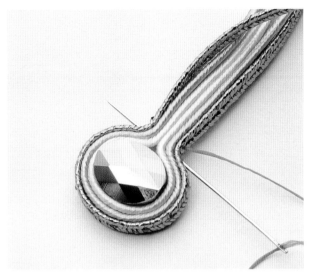

1   Glue the mini square beads and the mini oval beads to the beading foundation. When dry, cut around the beads. Thread the needle.

    Cut a 5½" (14cm) length of braid from each color. Make a closed wrap (page 15) with one mini oval bead, sewing the braids in the order A, B, C. Fix the braids together at the meeting point. Make a few stitches to secure them.

2   Sew out from the meeting point on either side and pick up a 4mm bicone bead. Divide the braids into two groups of three and bend three pieces of soutache over the bicone. Make a closed curve (page 20) around the bicone. Repeat on the other side with a second 4mm bicone. Cut off the remaining braids and apply glue to the braid ends.

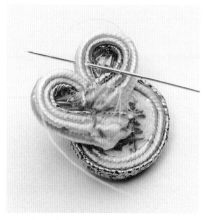

3 Pass the needle up through the meeting point and pick up a metal rose bead and a seed bead. Sew back into the base through the rose bead only. This will attach the rose to the top middle of the braids. Tie off the thread with several knots and clip the thread close.

4 Thread your needle with roughly 6" (15cm) of invisible thread. Pass the needle through the bottom of one curve roughly 1/16" (2mm) from where the two curves meet.

5 Pass the needle through the tear-drop's hole and take the needle back into the same curve. Lead the needle to the back of the other curve and sew out through the bottom of the curve roughly 1/16" (2mm) from where the two curves meet. Pass the needle through the teardrop's hole and take the needle back into the same curve. Repeat this several times to secure the teardrop to the base. Tie off the thread and clip close.

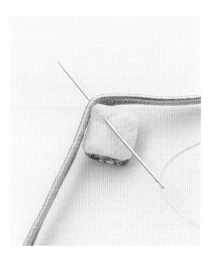

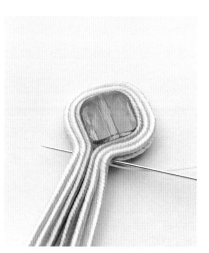

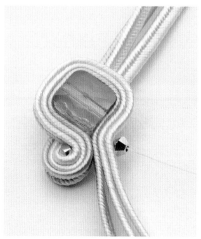

6 Cut two 5½" (14cm) braids from color A and one 5½" (14cm) braid from color B. Thread the needle with a thread that matches the braids. Make a closed wrap around one mini square bead, using the B-colored braid first.

7 Sew on the other two A-colored braids and fix the braids together at the meeting point.

8 Sew out on either side of the meeting point, pick up a B-colored bicone and make a closed curve. Lead the braids behind the work. Repeat the closed curve on the other side.

9 Cut off the remaining braids, apply glue to the ends and tie off the thread. Place the pieces on leather and trace around them; cut out the shapes.

Thread the needle with invisible thread. Pass the needle up through the top of the square bead, roughly $1/32$" (1mm) from the center. Add the ear wire and stitch back to the base $1/32$" (1mm) on the other side of center. Repeat several times to secure the ear wire.

10 Lead the needle through the back of the base and pass it through the meeting point below the square bead.

11 Fix a basket bead cap on top of the braids. Sew it on horizontally through the holes of the bead cap. Secure it with several stitches. Pass the needle down through the braids of either curve, in line with the bicone, and pick up an A-colored bicone.

12 Sew into the top of the oval bead element as shown. Secure with several stitches, then repeat with the second A-colored bicone as shown.

13 Glue the previously cut leather pieces to the back of the earring elements, using the technique on page 29. Repeat all steps for the second earring.

PINK *ring*

THE UNIQUE SHAPE AND THE FUNKY COLOR choices make this ring a stunning addition to your jewelry box. It's a colorful ring full of joy and happiness.

FINISHED SIZE

Approximately 1¼" × 1¼" (3.1cm × 3.1cm)

MATERIALS

soutache braids in four colors:

A: goldenrod, 6"(15cm)

B: light raspberry, 13½" (34cm)

C: dark raspberry, 13½" (34cm)

D: pastel yellow, 6" (15cm)

1 Swarovski xilion rose flatback, Ss34 (jet nut)

Swarovski bicone beads, 3mm, in two colors:

A: white opal, 2 beads

B: smoked topaz, 2 beads

15 rhinestones on a chain, 2.1mm wide (opaque turquoise)

1 ring base with 15mm × 11mm pad (gold tone)

beading foundation (Lacy's Stiff Stuff)

leather or ultrasuede for backing

thread and invisible thread

embroidery needle

tape measure

scissors

glue

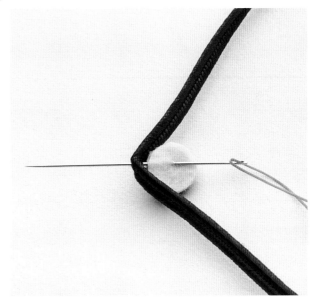

1 Glue the rose flatback to the beading foundation. When dry, cut around the bead. Thread the needle, cut the thread to a comfortable length and tie a knot at one end.

Cut two 6¾" (17cm) braids of colors B and C. Start to sew the C braid around the crystal through the foundation, but do not sew it on completely.

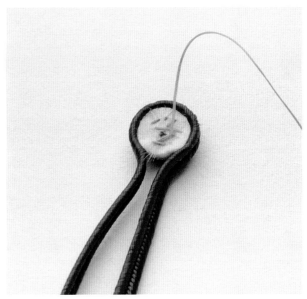

2 Finish sewing the braid roughly ⅛" (3mm) away from the starting point.

3 Sew on the other three braids in the order B, B, C, but don't fix them together at the meeting point. Instead, pass the needle through the pieces of braid on either side and pick up an A-colored bicone bead.

4 Sew through the opposite braids and repeat with several stitches to fix the bead between the two groups of braids.

5 Sew another A bicone bead between the braids. Then sew out from the second bicone on either side and pick up a B-colored bicone.

6 Bend four braids over the bicone and make a closed curve (page 20). Lead the braids behind the work and cut off the ends; apply glue to the braid ends. Add a second B bicone to the other side and make a closed curve. Tie off the thread with several knots and clip close.

7 Thread the needle with invisible thread. Cut a 6" (15cm) braid of colors A and D. With the piece face down, pass the needle through the braids of the right curve, above the top white opal bicone. Sew through the A braid, leaving a tail of 3/8"–5/8" (1cm–1.6cm).

8 Sew the A braid around the curve, then sew on the D braid. Make a curve with the braids, as shown. Pass the needle through the braids on both sides of the curve, but do not pull the thread tight.

9   Place one rhinestone through the thread between the braids. Sew back through the braids between the first two segments of the rhinestone chain. Secure with several stitches so the thread is both above and below the rhinestone connection (page 21).

10 Continue to sew the rhinestone chain between the braids, curving the braids back along the yellow curve and behind the work. Cut off the remaining braids and apply glue to the braid ends. Tie off the thread and clip close. Place the piece on the leather, trace around it and cut out the shape.

11 Mark and cut two slits for the ring base. The ring base must be behind the rhinestone chain part of the piece.

12 Insert the ring base through the slits from the back side of the leather. Secure the leather to the ring base with a little glue.

13 Apply a thin coat of glue to the back of the rhinestone chain part of the piece and glue it to the part of the leather with the ring base. Carefully glue the rest of the leather to the back of the work.

APOLLO *pendant*

GLAMORIZE YOUR DESK-TO-DINNER LOOK with this shimmering pendant. Rows of feminine crystal and the braided leather give this shiny pendant a sense of ultramodern elegance.

FINISHED SIZE

Approximately 32½" (83cm); pendant is approximately 3¾" × 2" (9.5cm × 5.1cm), including drop

MATERIALS

soutache braids in two colors:

A: sage green, 80¾" (205cm)

B: beige, 98½" (250cm)

18 Swarovski bicone beads, 4mm (dark red coral)

2 Swarovski bicone beads, 6mm (sand opal)

1 Swarovski oval fancy stone, 14mm × 10mm (iridescent green)

8 Swarovski bicone beads, 3mm (sand opal)

1 Swarovski square fancy stone, 12mm (iridescent green)

4 seed beads, 15/0 (matte color iris gray)

2 Swarovski teardrop pendants, 16mm (iridescent green)

2 Czech druk round beads, 8mm (beige gold picasso)

1 closed ring, 27mm (antique brass)

38" (15cm) braided leather, 4mm (natural)

beading foundation (Lacy's Stiff Stuff)

leather or ultrasuede for backing

thread and invisible thread

embroidery needle

tape measure

scissors

glue

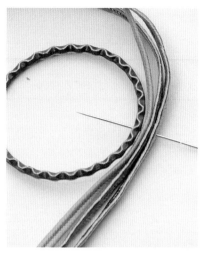

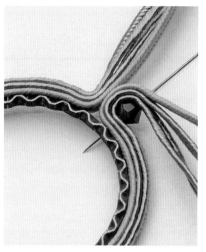

1 Thread the needle with invisible thread. Cut two 12" (30cm) braids of color A and one 12" (30cm) braid of color B. Attach the soutache around the closed ring (page 17) in the following order, starting from the inside: B, A, A.

2 Fix the braids together at the meeting point with several stitches. Pass the needle up through the braids roughly ⅛" (3mm) from the meeting point on either side. Pick up a 4mm bicone.

3 Divide the braids into two groups of three; bend one group over the bicone. Pass the needle up through these braids, then take the needle down through the braids and the bicone at a point just a little farther down the base; pull the needle out completely.

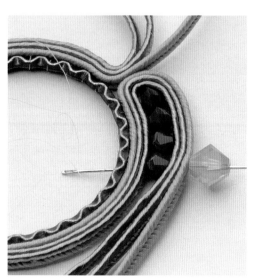

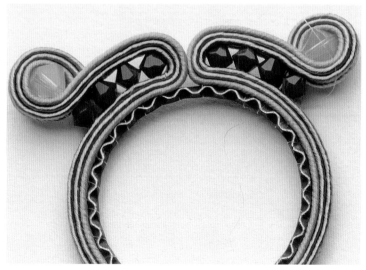

4 Sew three more bicone beads in the same way (page 18). Lead the needle through the last bicone and the braids and pick up a 6mm bicone bead.

5 Make a closed curve (page 20) around the 6mm bicone. Repeat steps 2–5 on the other side. Cut off the remaining braids and apply glue to the ends. Tie off the thread with several knots and clip close.

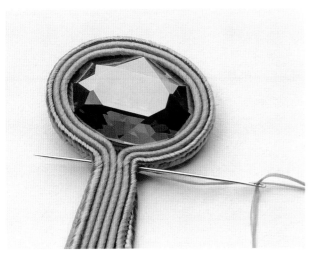 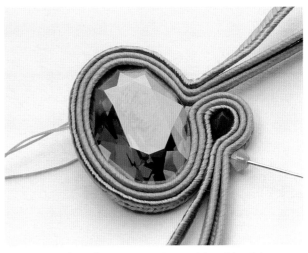

6 Glue the oval and square fancy stones to the beading foundation following the technique on page 10. When dry, cut around the stones. Cut two 7" (18cm) braids from color B and one 7" (18cm) braid from color A. Thread your needle, cut the thread to a comfortable length and tie a knot at one end.

Make a closed wrap (page 15) around the oval stone with the braids in the order B, B, A. Fix the braids together at the meeting point. Make a few stitches to secure them.

7 Sew out from the meeting point on either side, pick up a 4mm bicone bead and make an open curve (page 19) around it using three braids. Sew the upper braids to the base at one point and pass the needle up through this point. Pick up a 3mm bicone bead.

  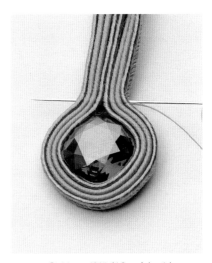

8 Make a closed curve around the 3mm bicone. Repeat steps 7–8 on the other side. Cut off the remaining braids and apply glue to the ends. Take the needle back to the meeting point and sew a 3mm bicone bead onto the top of the braids in the middle.

9 Referring to the photo, sew the oval stone element to the middle bottom of the closed ring. Tie off the thread with several knots and clip close.

10 Cut two 4¾" (12cm) braids from colors A and B. Thread the needle. Make a closed wrap around the square fancy stone. Use the braids in this order: A, B, B, A. Fix the braids together at the meeting point. Make a few stitches to secure them.

11 Fix this element to the back of the work, opposite the oval stone. Refer to the photo. Tie off the thread with several knots and clip close.

12 Trim the braid ends to below the ring and apply glue to the ends.

Thread the needle with invisible thread. Pass the needle through the braids behind the outer curve of the oval. Pass the needle through the back side of the base through the back of the braided leather, leaving a tail of 1¾" (4.4cm). At almost the same point, take the needle back through the leather farther down the base.

13 Sew the leather braid behind the oval stone. Start and finish the leather braid behind the first 4mm bicones. Keep your stitches on the back of the work. Cut off the excess leather braid and apply a thin coat of glue to the ends.

14 Pass the needle up from the back of the work, under the square stone and through the initial meeting point. Pick up three seed beads.

15 Pick up a teardrop pendant and sew back through the seed beads, back to the base. Secure with several stitches. Lead the needle out from the stem of the square stone element. Sew a 3mm bicone bead to the middle top of the braids.

16 Cut a 23¾" (60cm) braid of color B, bend it in half and fix it to the back of the square stone at the center top. Tie off the thread with several knots and clip close.

17 Thread the needle, cut about 8" (20cm) of invisible thread and tie a knot at one end. Sew out from the middle bottom of the base and fix a seed bead and a teardrop pendant to the base. Tie off the thread with several knots and clip close.

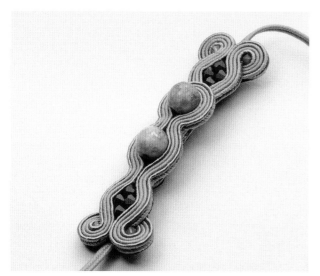

18 Cut four 10" (25cm) braids of colors A and B. Align and stack the braids in this order for each half of the clasp: A, B, B, A. Make a hand-embroidered clasp (page 23) using two druk round beads on top of the braids, 4mm bicone beads between the braids in diamond shapes (page 28) and 3mm bicone beads for the curves. Sew one half of the clasp to each of the braid ends.

19 Cover the back of the work with leather (page 29).

CAPRICE *earrings*

THESE EARRINGS remind me of drinking cold tea on the front porch on a hot Southern summer night.

FINISHED SIZE

Approximately 3¾" × 1½" (9.5cm × 3.5cm), including drop

MATERIALS

soutache braids in three colors:

    A: goldenrod, 27½" (70cm)

    B: golden orange, 59" (150cm)

    C: lime, 75" (190cm)

2 Swarovski square fancy stones, 12mm (crystal astral pink)

20 rhinestones in a cup chain, 3mm (aqua opal)

Swarovski bicone beads, 3mm, in two colors:

    A: tangerine, 4 beads

    B: crystal metallic light gold, 2 beads

4 Swarovski navettes, 10mm × 5mm (crystal astral pink)

Swarovski bicone beads, 4mm, in two colors:

    A: tangerine, 6 beads

    B: sand opal, 4 beads

4 metal watermelon beads, 8mm (antique bronze)

2 seed beads, 15/0 (metallic gold)

2 Swarovski teardrop pendants, 16mm (crystal copper)

4 settings for Swarovski navette stones

2 closed rings, 7mm (antique brass)

2 basket bead caps, 6mm (antique brass)

2 ear studs (copper)

beading foundation (Lacy's Stiff Stuff)

leather or ultrasuede for backing

thread and invisible thread

embroidery needle

tape measure

scissors

glue

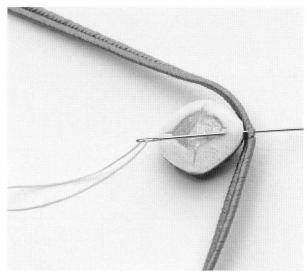

1 Thread the needle and cut the thread to a comfortable length. Glue the square stone to the beading foundation using the technique on page 10. When dry, cut around the stone. Cut one 6¼" (16cm) braid from each color. Make a closed wrap (page 15), starting with the B braid.

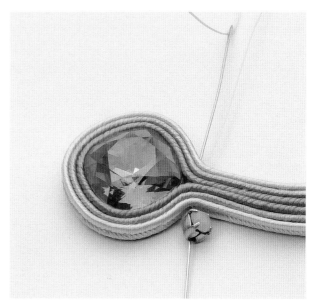

2 Sew on the A braid and the C braid. Fix the braids together at the meeting point. Make a few stitches to secure. Cut one rhinestone from the cup chain and pass the needle through the meeting point and through the little hole of the stone setting.

3 Divide the braids into two groups of three; bend three braids over the rhinestone. Make a closed curve (page 20) around the rhinestone. Repeat on the other side. Cut off the remaining braids and apply glue to the ends.

Pass the needle up through the braids at the meeting point and sew a 3mm B-colored bicone to the top of the braids.

4 Cut two 3" (8cm) braids from color C and attach them to the back of the element behind the right curve.

5 Stitch the braids completely around this curve. When you're making the other earring in this pair, sew the C braids around the opposite curve.

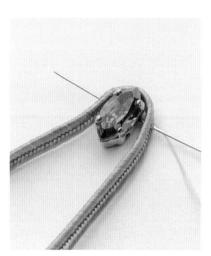

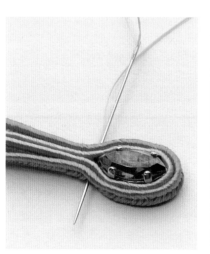

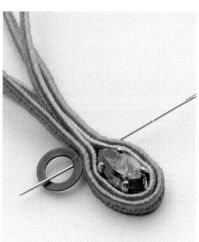

6 Place the navette stones into the settings. Cut a 7" (18cm) braid from colors A and B. Apply the A braid around the navette through the setting holes. Use several stitches to secure the braid.

7 Sew on the B braid and fix the braids together at the meeting point with several stitches. Tie off the thread with several knots and clip close.

8 Thread the needle with invisible thread. Sew out from the meeting point on the same side as the curve in step 5 and align the braids with the closed ring. Sew through the meeting point and insert the needle below the closed ring.

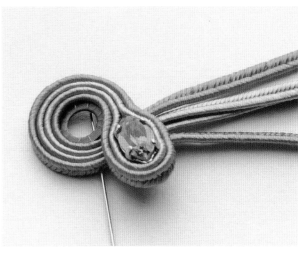

9   Pass the needle back through the braid, above the closed ring. Bring the needle back through the braids, roughly ⅛" (3mm) away from the first stitch and keep stitching the braids all the way around the ring. Lead the braids behind the work and fix them to the back with several stitches.

10   Cut two 4¾" (12cm) braids from color C and one 4¾" (12cm) braid from color B. Pass the needle up through the braids next to the navette stone and, at almost the same point, take the needle back, but don't pull the thread completely. This forms a loop for the first stone of the rhinestone chain.

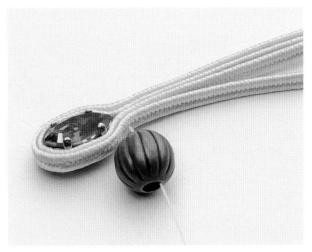

11   Apply eight pieces of rhinestone chain between the braids (page 21) around the closed ring curve. Use the braids in the order C, C, B. Pass the needle up from the base, behind the last stone of the rhinestone chain, and pick up a 4mm B-colored bicone bead.

Make a closed curve around the bicone. Tie off the thread with several knots, clip close and cut off the remaining braids. Apply a thin coat of glue to the ends.

12   Thread your needle. Cut two 7" (18cm) braids from color C and apply them around a second navette through the setting holes. Sew the braids together at the meeting point. Sew out the side as shown. Pick up an 8mm metal bead.

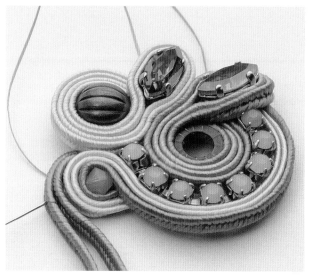

13 Make a closed curve around the metal bead. Fix this element to the top of the previous element as shown. Sew the two navette elements together through the braids. Attach the curve of the metal bead to the curve of the bicone as well.

14 Cut two 2½" (6cm) braids from color B and sew them around the 4mm bicone curve. Start stitching them from behind the metal bead curve and sew the other ends to the back of the base piece.

15 Sew one 3mm A-colored bicone on top of the meeting point of each navette bead.

16 Cut a 6" (15cm) braid from color B and bend it in half. Stitch the bent end to the base under the rhinestone nearest the navette elements.

17 Sew the bent braid along four of the rhinestones. Pass the needle out through the braids. Pick up a 4mm B-colored bicone.

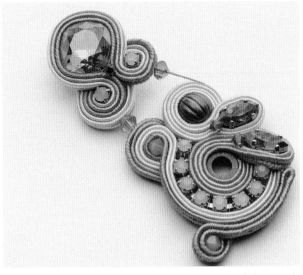

18 Make a closed curve around the bicone. Cut off the remaining braids and apply glue to the ends.
    Make the second earring. Remember that the elements and curves must mirror those of the first earring.

19 Place the pieces on the leather, trace around them and cut out the shapes.
    Connect the main elements to the square stone elements using invisible thread and two 4mm A-colored bicone beads as shown.

20 Lead the needle down and pass it through the braids between the second and third stones of the rhinestone chain. Pick up a seed bead, a 4mm A-colored bicone, a metal bead, a basket bead cap and a teardrop pendant. Stitch back through the all beads and farther up the base. Secure these beads to the base with several stitches. Repeat for the second earring.

21 Use a needle to pierce a hole in the leather backing behind the square stone. From the wrong side of the leather, pass the ear stud through the hole. Apply a thin coat of glue on the wrong side of the leather to secure the stud.

22 Cover the back of the work with the leather pieces (page 29).

NOTE
*The materials listed will
make a bracelet 7½"
(19cm) long. If you wish to
make it longer, you will need
more 8mm fire-polished
beads. Periodically measure
the length of the bracelet as
you work and make adjust-
ments as needed.*

AMERICA *bracelet*

IN THIS MIXED-TEXTURE BRACELET, the softness of the fabric and the hardness of the central piece create an eclectic look that will definitely attract attention!

FINISHED SIZE Approximately 7½" (19cm)

MATERIALS

soutache braids in three colors:

    A: purple, 69" (175cm)

    B: rust, 82¾" (210cm)

    C: gold, 59" (150cm)

2 Czech flat rectangle beads, 12mm (green with gold edge)

20 Czech fire-polished beads, 3mm (umber)

12 rhinestones in a chain, 2.5mm wide (pink opal)

2 Czech fire-polished beads, 4mm (umber AB)

2 Swarovski bicone beads, 3mm (rose opal)

3 Miyuki tila beads, 5mm (matte metallic gold)

1 coin bead, 8mm (purple marble)

4 Czech fire-polished beads, 8mm (transparent peach)

1 round bead, 4mm (purple marble)

5 seed beads, 15/0 (crystal-lined green)

2 Czech glass coin beads, 10mm (brown toffee)

beading foundation (Lacy's Stiff Stuff)

leather or ultrasuede for backing

thread and invisible thread

embroidery needle

tape measure

scissors

glue

1 Glue the flat rectangle beads to the beading foundation. When dry, cut around the beads. Cut a 6" (15cm) braid from each color. Thread the needle and tie a knot at one end.

Make a closed wrap (page 15) using one rectangle bead and the B braid. Sew on the C braid and the A braid and fix them together at the meeting point. Make a few stitches to secure them.

2 Sew out on one side of the meeting point, pick up a 3mm fire-polished bead and make a closed curve (page 20) with three of the braids.

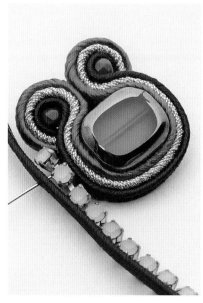

3 Repeat on the other side with the remaining three braids and another 3mm fire-polished bead. Cut off the remaining braids. Apply glue to the braid ends, tie off the thread with several knots and clip close.

Thread your needle with invisible thread. Cut a 5¼" (13cm) braid of each color. Bring the needle out from the base, under one closed curve, and take the needle back into the base at almost the same point. Do not pull the thread completely. Place the first rhinestone in the chain through the loop. Attach the rhinestone chain between the braids (page 21) around the base, using the A braid first.

4 After the rhinestone chain and the braid have been applied, sew on the other two braids in the order C, B.

5 Lead the braids behind the base and cut off the remaining braids. Apply glue to the ends, tie off the thread with several knots and clip close.

Thread your needle. Cut an 8" (20cm) braid of each color. Pass the needle out the center bottom of the base. Pick up a 3mm fire-polished bead and pass the needle through the middle of the A braid.

6 Stitch a row of 3mm fire-polished beads to the bottom of the piece (page 18). Sew five beads to the left of the first bead and five to the right, for a total of eleven beads. Then sew on the C and B braids.

Pass the needle through the last fire-polished bead on either side, pick up a 4mm fire-polished bead and make an open curve around it (page 19).

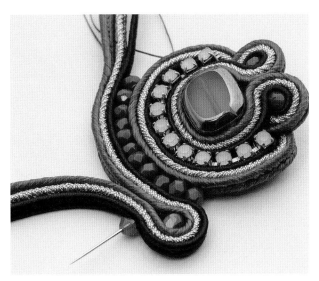

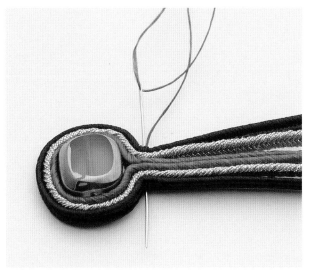

7 Sew out from the point where the upper braids of the curve have been sewn to the base and pick up a bicone. Make a closed curve around it.

Repeat these two curves on the other end of the row of 3mm beads. Lead the braids behind the base and cut off the remaining braids. Apply glue to the ends, tie off the thread with several knots and clip close.

8 Thread the needle and cut a 5¼" (13cm) braid of each color. Make a closed wrap using the second rectangle bead and the B braid. Sew on the other two braids in the order C, A. Fix them together at the meeting point. Make a few stitches to secure them.

9 Sew this element to the bottom of the base of the main element between the two bicone curves. Sew it to the curves as well. Cut off the remaining braids and apply glue to the ends.

10 Cut two 4¾" (12cm) A braids and one 4¾" (12cm) B braid. Bring the needle out at the bottom of the second rectangle element, pick up a tila bead and go through the middle of the A braid. Use both holes of the tila bead to attach it to the rectangle element and the A braid.

11 Sew one tila bead on each side of the first bead in the same way. Lead the braids alongside the end tila beads and sew them to the back of the base. Cut off the remaining braids and apply glue to the braid ends. Tie off the thread with several knots and clip close.

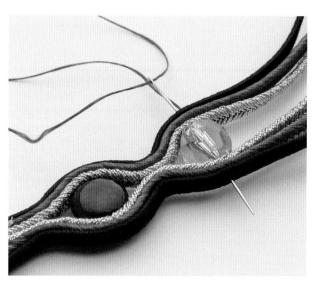

12 Thread your needle and cut two 4" (10cm) braids of each color. Align and stack the braids in this order: A, B, C, C, B, A. Sew all the braids together at one point, covering the knot (page 16, step 1). Fix the 8mm coin bead between the braids using the open wrap technique (page 14).

13 Using the same technique, fix an 8mm fire-polished bead between the braids.

Lead the needle up a few stitches (roughly the same distance as above the bead) on either side and fix all the braids together below the bead. This is one "bend."

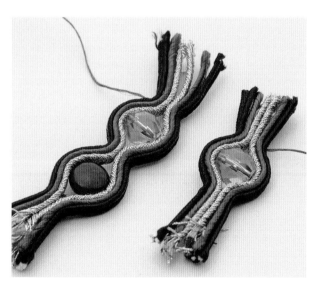

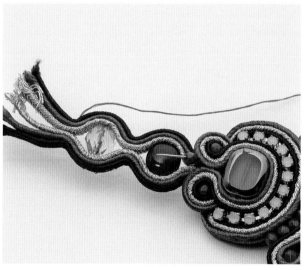

14 Measure your bracelet. My bracelet is 7½" (19cm) long. If you wish to make yours longer, you will need one more 8mm fire-polished bead and double the length of braids mentioned below.

Thread the needle and cut two 3¼" (8cm) braids of each color. Align and stack the braids in this order: A, B, C, C, B, A. Use the open wrap technique to fix one (or two) 8mm fire-polished bead(s) between the braids. Cover the knot. Now you have two bends.

15 Sew the first bend to the base above the two curves from steps 2 and 3. Make a few stitches to secure them together. Sew a 3mm fire-polished bead on top of the braids between the two curves.

16 Lead the needle down and fix the round bead at the meeting point above the first rectangle bead. Make several stitches to secure it.

17 Lead the needle down to the next rectangle bead and sew five seed beads above the bead.

Sew the second bend to the base on this side. Cut off the remaining braids and apply glue to the ends. Tie off the thread with several knots and clip close.

18 Thread the needle, cut the thread to a comfortable length and tie a knot at one end. Cut four 10" (25cm) B braids and two 10" (25cm) A and C braids. Align the braids and make two stacks in this order: B, C, A, B. Make a hand-embroidered clasp (page 23) using the 8mm fire-polished beads on top of the braids, the 10mm coin beads between the braids and the 3mm fire-polished beads for the curves and on top of the meeting points above the coin beads.

19 Sew one clasp element to the end of each bend. Cover the back of the work with leather (page 29) to finish.

MEXICO *pendant*

MEXICO IS FULL OF BEAUTIFUL COLORS, and so is this pendant. The soutache braids, beads and vibrant tassel make a bold statement that will make you smile.

FINISHED SIZE

Approximately 25½" (64.7cm) long, excluding tassel; pendant is approximately 3" × 2¼" (7.2cm × 5.8cm)

MATERIALS

soutache braids in four colors:

A: purple, 104¼" (265cm)

B: orange, 75" (190cm)

C: silver gray, 41¼" (105cm)

D: lemon, 23¾" (60cm)

1 Czech oval table-cut bead, 11mm × 9mm (cream picasso)

18 rhinestones in a cup chain, 2.5mm wide (opaque yellow)

15/0 seed beads in two colors:

A: gold-lined rainbow black diamond, 40 beads

B: opaque red, 60 beads

2 Toho triangle beads, 2.2mm (crystal yellow-lined)

Czech fire-polished beads, 3mm, in two colors:

A: jet picasso, 6 beads

B: opaque green, 1 bead

20 rhinestones in a chain, 2.1mm wide (opaque coral)

1 Czech rectangle table-cut bead, 12mm × 8mm (orange travertine)

30 Miyuki twisted bugle beads, 6mm (matte metallic patina iris)

3 Czech fire-polished beads, 4mm (opaque red)

8 Swarovski crystal round beads, 4mm (neon yellow)

1 Czech African bicone bead, 11mm (green bottle glass and rustic picasso)

3 coin beads, 8mm (purple marble)

2 Czech faceted beads, 8mm × 6mm (opaque burnt orange picasso)

1 basket bead cap, 6mm (antique silver)

1 flower bead cap, 5mm (copper)

8 pieces of fringe trim, 10" (25cm) each, for tassel

beading foundation (Lacy's Stiff Stuff)

leather or ultrasuede for backing

thread and invisible thread

embroidery needle

tape measure

scissors

glue

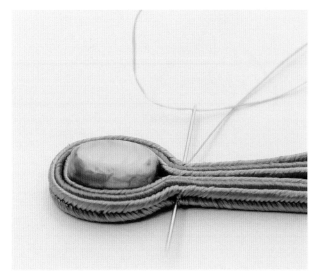

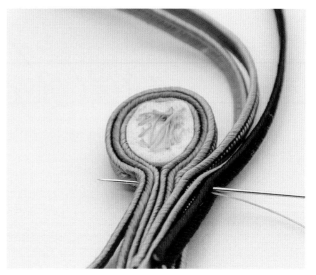

1 Glue the oval table-cut bead and the rectangle bead to the beading foundation. When dry, cut around the beads. Cut a 4¾" (12cm) braid from color B and two 4¾" (12cm) braids from color C. Thread your needle and tie a knot at one end.

Make a closed wrap (page 15) using the oval bead and one C braid. Sew on the other two braids, first B and then C, and fix them together at the meeting point. Make a few stitches to secure them.

2 Cut a 4" (10cm) braid from color A and two 4" (10cm) braids from color C. Sew out one side of the meeting point and the pass the needle through the braids in the following order: C, C, A.

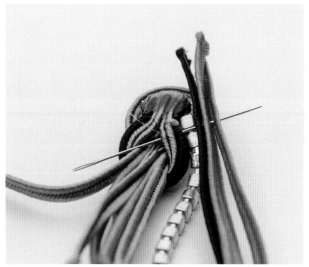

3 Attach the braids above the base (page 25). Cut off the remaining braids and apply glue to the ends. Tie off the thread with several knots and clip close. Thread your needle with invisible thread. Bring the needle out from the base and take the needle back at almost the same point. Do not pull the thread completely. This will form a loop.

4 Cut a 4¾" (12cm) braid from color A and two 4¾" (12cm) braids from color B. Attach approximately twelve 2.5mm rhinestones from the chain between the braids (pages 21–22). Start and finish stitching the rhinestone chain at the back of the base. Use the braids in the following order: A, B, B.

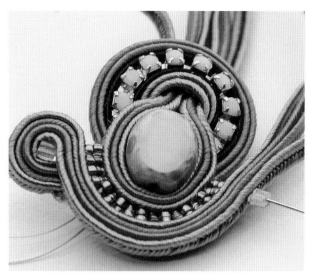

5 Cut off the remaining braids and apply glue to the ends. Cut two 6" (15cm) braids from colors B and C. At the end of the oval bead, thread on two A-colored seed beads and the braids in the order C, B, B, C. Start sewing a row of stacked seed beads to the bottom of the element (page 18).

6 Sew eight stacks of two beads to the right of the first two beads and eight stacks to the left of the first two beads. Pass the needle through the last row of seed beads, pick up a triangle bead and make a closed curve (page 20). Repeat on the other end of the row of seed beads.

7 Cut off the remaining braids and apply glue to the ends.
Cut two 4" (10cm) braids of color A. Stack the braids and sew them to the back of the work and then around the triangle bead curve.

8 At the end of the curve, pass the needle up through the braids, next to the end of the row of seed beads. Pick up a jet picasso 3mm fire-polished bead.

9 Make a closed curve around the jet picasso bead. Add one more stack of A-colored seed beads between the braids if needed to fill in the space at the end of the row.
Repeat steps 7–9 on the other side of the row of seed beads. Tie off the thread with several knots and clip close.

10 Cut 4" (10cm) braids from colors A, C and D. Thread your needle with invisible thread. Pass the needle through the base on either side of the 2.5mm rhinestone curve and under the jet picasso curve. With the braids in the order D, C, A, sew the 2.1mm rhinestone chain between the braids around the previous rhinestone chain section.

11 Sew the 3mm B-colored fire-polished bead below the oval bead. Add a row of four A-colored seed beads below the fire-polished bead, then add a second row of four A-colored seed beads. Tie off the thread with several knots, clip close and cut off all remaining braids. Apply a thin coat of glue to the braid ends.

12 Cut a 4" (10cm) braid from colors A, B and D; cut two 4" (10cm) braids from color C. Make a closed wrap around the rectangle bead with the braids in the order A, C, C, D, B.

13 Attach this element to the bottom of the previous element, between the two triangle bead curves.

14 Cut a 6" (15cm) braid from color A and two 6" (15cm) braids from color B. Stitch a row of bugle beads to the top of one triangle bead curve, butting the first bugle bead up to the rectangle bead braids. Use the braids in the order B, B, A and leave a 1¼" (3cm) tail at the end of the braid.

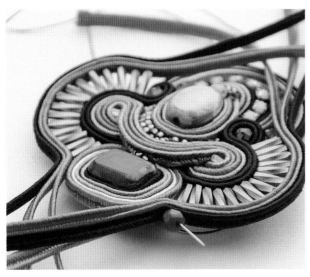

15 Sew fifteen bugle beads into this row. Stitch the braids to the rectangle bead braids with several stitches. Repeat steps 14–15 around the second triangle bead curve.

Lead the needle to where the braids meet the rectangle bead on one side. Pick up a red 4mm fire-polished bead. Make a closed curve around the bead.

16 Repeat, making a closed curve around a red 4mm fire-polished bead on the other side of the rectangle bead.

Lead the needle through the back of the work to the farthest bugle bead on one side. Sew the upper braids to the 2.1mm rhinestone braids with several stitches. Lead the needle out and pick up a crystal round bead. Make a closed curve around the bead. Cut off the remaining braids and apply glue to the ends.

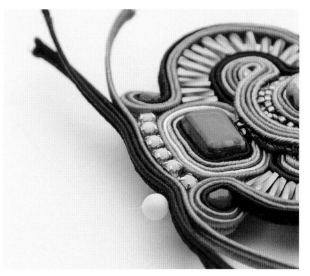

17 Repeat, making a closed curve around a crystal round bead on the other side of the 2.1mm rhinestones. Tie off the thread with several knots and clip close.

Thread your needle with invisible thread, cut a 4¾" (12cm) braid from color B and two 4¾" (12cm) braids from color A. Stack the braids in the order B, A, A. Leaving a 1½" (4cm) tail, use the braids to sew six 2.5mm rhinestones between the red 4mm fire-polished bead curves.

18 After you've applied the rhinestone chain, fix the lower braids to the red fire-polished curve with several stitches. Lead the needle out to the braids at one end of the rhinestone chain. Pick up a crystal round bead and make a closed curve around it.

19 Repeat the closed curve on the other side. Tie off the thread with several knots, clip close and cut off all remaining braids. Apply a thin coat of glue to the braid ends.

20 Group six of the fringe trim pieces together and fold in the middle. Tie the seventh length of trim to the fold with a knot.

21 Roughly ¼" (6mm) from the fold, tie a knot around the trim with the last piece of fringe trim.

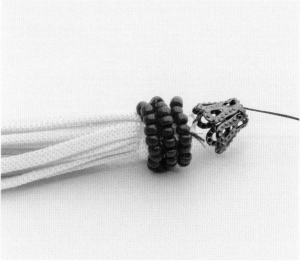

22 Thread your needle and cut the thread to a comfortable length. Tie a knot in one end of the thread. Sew out from the fringe base, pick up three B-colored seed beads and sew back through the base. Bring the needle out in front of the first row of seed beads, pass the needle through the beads, pick up three more seed beads and sew back through the base. Repeat these steps all the way around the fringe trim.

23 Sew two more rows of B-colored seed beads above the first, over the fringe base. Lead the needle out the top and pick up the basket bead cap.

24 After the bead cap, pick up a B-colored seed bead, the bicone bead, a B-colored seed bead and one coin bead. Pick up the flower bead cap so the cup is facing away from the coin bead. Attach the flower bead cap to the main element, centered between the bottom two crystal round beads. Make a few stitches to secure the tassel element to the base.

25 Thread your needle with invisible thread. Cut an 18" (46cm) braid of color A and bend it in half. Attach the folded end to the back top of the base, centering it along the 2.1mm rhinestone braids. Attach a red 4mm fire-polished bead to the top of the braids at the same point. Secure with several stitches. This is the chain of the pendant.

26 Cut two 8" (20cm) braids from colors B and D and four 8" (20cm) braids from color A. Make two stacks of the braids in the order A, B, D, A. Make a hand-embroidered clasp (pages 23–24), using the two 8mm × 6mm faceted beads on top of the braids, two coin beads between the braids and crystal round beads for the curves. Sew jet picasso fire-polished beads on top of the meeting points. Sew one chain end to the back of each clasp piece.

27 Cover the back of the work with leather (page 29) to finish the piece.

INDIA *choker*

MAKE A DESIGN MORE INTERESTING by mixing things up. The combination of shiny crystals, colorful chains and the metallic soutache creates a choker that's elegant and folksy at the same time.

FINISHED SIZE

Approximately 14½" (37cm) long; pendant is approximately 2¼" × 2" (5.7cm × 5.2cm)

MATERIALS

soutache braids in five colors:

    A: metallic copper, 90¾" (230cm)

    B: deep beige, 82¾" (210cm)

    C: orange, 90¾" (230cm)

    D: dark brown, 12" (30cm)

    E: turquoise, 29½" (75cm)

1 Swarovski oval fancy stone, 18mm × 13mm (padparadscha)

3 Swarovski xilion rose flatbacks, Ss34 (jet nut)

1 Miyuki tila bead, 5mm (matte metallic gold)

rhinestone chain, 2.1mm wide, in two colors:

    turquoise, 22–24 stones

    chalk white, 42–44 stones

4 Czech renaissance beads, 6mm (red picasso)

20 Swarovski bicone beads, 3mm (crystal rose gold)

16 Swarovski bicone beads, 4mm (crystal rose gold)

2 Czech glass fluted cathedral beads, 9mm (red picasso)

12 Swarovski round beads, 4mm (padparadscha)

2 Swarovski round pearls, 4mm (brown)

1 Swarovski oval fancy stone, 14mm × 10mm (padparadscha)

8 seed beads, 15/0 (crystal gold bronze)

2 closed rings, 12mm (raw brass)

4¾" (12cm) box chain, 3mm (orange)

8 flower bead caps, 5mm (copper)

beading foundation (Lacy's Stiff Stuff)

leather or ultrasuede for backing

thread and invisible thread

embroidery needle

tape measure

scissors

glue

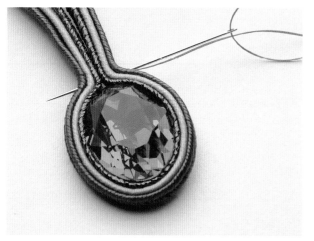

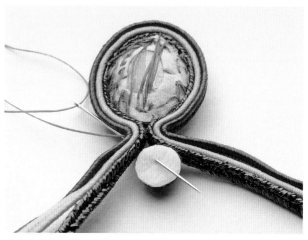

1 Glue the two oval fancy stones to the beading foundation using the technique on pages 10–11. Glue the flatbacks to the beading foundation. When dry, cut around the beads. Cut an 8" (20cm) braid from colors A, B and C.

Thread the needle and make a closed wrap (page 15) using the 18mm × 13mm oval stone and the A braid. Sew on the other two braids in the order B, C. Fix them together at the meeting point. Make a few stitches to secure them.

2 Divide the braids into two groups of three. Pass the needle up through one side, roughly ⅛" (3mm) away from the meeting point. Stitch through the foundation at the back of one flatback bead and sew it between the braids.

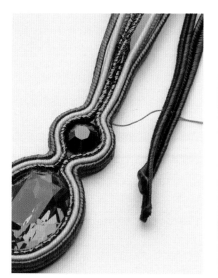

3 Sew all the braids together at the meeting point below the flatback bead with several stitches.

Cut two 3" (7cm) braids of color D. Sew out from the meeting point and pass the needle through the two D braids, leaving a ¾" (2cm) tail.

4 Sew the two D braids above the base using the first six steps of the technique on page 25.

5 Make a closed curve without beads (page 20) around the D braids on both sides by bending the A, B and C braids over the D braids. Lead the braids behind the base. Cut off all remaining braids and apply a thin coat of glue to the braid ends. Tie off the thread with several knots and clip close.

6 Thread the needle with invisible thread. Pass the needle up through the braids above the oval stone and sew a tila bead on top of the braids at the meeting point.

7 Cut a 7" (18cm) braid from colors A, B and C. Still using invisible thread, bring the needle out from the base roughly ⅛" (3mm) from the meeting point between the oval stone and the flatback bead. Insert the needle at almost the same point, but do not pull the thread completely; make a loop instead. Place the first A-colored rhinestone through the loop. Apply the rhinestone chain (page 21) between the B braid and the base.

8 Sew on the other two braids in the order A, C. Bring the braid end to the back of the piece. Cut off the excess braids and apply a thin coat of glue to the ends.

9 With invisible thread, sew the box chain around the base, threading the needle through the boxes.

10 Cut a 8¾" (22cm) braid from colors A, B and C. Sew the braids around the box chain in the order A, B, C. Cut off the remaining braids and apply a thin coat of glue to the ends. Tie off the thread with several knots and clip close.

11 Cut a 9" (23cm) braid from colors A, C and E. Thread the needle with invisible thread and bring the needle out from the base, next to one of the closed curves. At almost the same point, insert the needle, but do not pull the thread completely; make a loop instead. Place the first B-colored rhinestone through the loop. Apply the rhinestone chain between the E braid and the base.

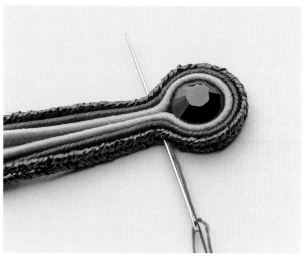

12 Sew on the other two braids in the order C, A. With the braids at the back of the piece, cut off the excess braids and apply a thin coat of glue to the ends. Tie off the thread with several knots and clip close.

Pass the needle up through the braids above the flatback bead and sew a 3mm bicone on top of the braids at the meeting point. This is the first element of the choker.

Tie off the threads. Cut off the excess braids and apply glue to the ends.

13 Thread your needle and tie a knot at one end. Cut a 15¾" (40cm) braid from colors A, B and C. Make a closed wrap with one flatback bead and the B braid. Sew on the other two braids in the order C, A. Fix them together at the meeting point. Make a few stitches to secure them.

Note: For a choker chain longer than 14½" (37cm), cut your braids longer than instructed above.

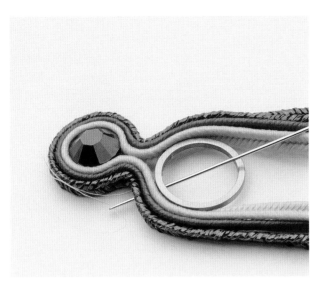

14 Thread the needle with invisible thread. Divide the braids into two groups of three. Pass the needle through on one side, roughly ¼" (6mm) from the meeting point. Sew both groups of braids around the closed ring (page 17).

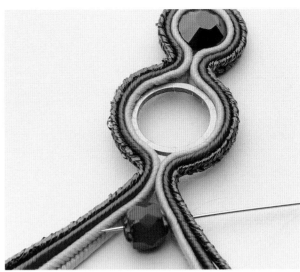

15 Sew all the braids together below the closed ring with several stitches. Divide the braids into two groups again and pass the needle through on one side, roughly ⅜" (8mm) from the meeting point. Insert the needle back through the braids, pick up a cathedral bead and insert the needle through the braids on the opposite side.

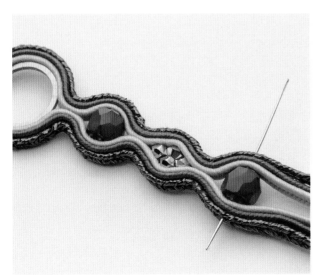

16 Make several stitches through the braids and the bead to secure them together. Lead the needle a few stitches down either group of braids to roughly the same distance as above the bead. Fix all the braids together below the bead.

Sew four 3mm bicone beads between the braids using the technique for making diamond shapes (page 28). Sew all the braids together below the diamond shape with several stitches. Divide the braids into two groups again and insert the needle out through either group roughly ⅜" (8mm) from the meeting point. Insert the needle back through the braids, pick up a cathedral bead and insert the needle through the braids on the opposite side.

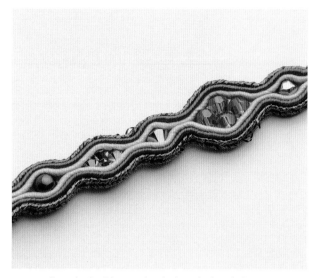

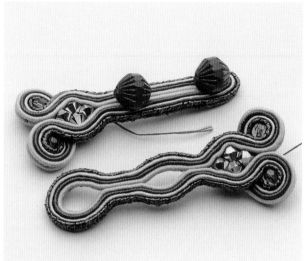

17 Sew the braids together below the bead. Sew a 4mm bicone between the braids, then sew a 4mm round bead in diamond shape. Following the same technique, add a 4mm bicone, then sew four 3mm bicones in diamond shape. Sew a 4mm pearl between the braids. This is your second element. Repeat steps 13–17 to make a third element.

18 Thread the needle. Cut two 10" (25cm) braids of colors A, B, C and E. Align the braids and make two stacks in this order: B, C, E, A. Make a hand-embroidered clasp (page 23) using cathedral beads on top of the braids, 4mm bicone beads in a diamond shape between the braids and 4mm round beads for the curves. Cut off the remaining braids and apply a thin coat of glue to the ends. Tie off the thread with several knots and clip close.

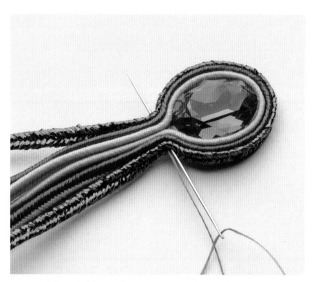

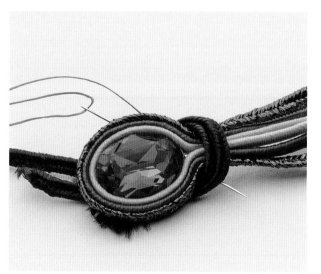

19 Thread the needle and cut a 6" (15cm) braid from colors A, B and C. Using the 14mm × 10mm oval fancy stone and the B braid, make a closed wrap. Sew on the other two braids in the order C, A. Fix them together at the meeting point. Make a few stitches to secure them.

20 Cut two 3" (7cm) braids of color D. Sew out from the meeting point and pass the needle through the braids, leaving a tail roughly ¾" (2cm) long. Sew the two D braids above the base using the first six steps of the technique on page 25.

21 Make a closed curve without beads (page 20) around the D braids on both sides by bending the A, B and C braids over the D braids. Lead the braids behind the base. Cut off all remaining braids and apply a thin coat of glue to the ends. Tie off the thread with several knots and clip close.

Pass the needle up through the meeting point, under the two D braids, and sew a 3mm bicone on top of the braids. Fix it several times and tie off the thread with several knots, then clip close. This is the fourth element.

22 Thread the needle with invisible thread. Fix the second and third elements on the sides of the fourth element using a flower bead cap, a 3mm bicone and a seed bead. Connect the elements with a second string of beads, angling down to the closed curves of the fourth element. This time use a seed bead, a 4mm bicone and a flower bead cap.

23 Fix the first element to the fourth element, connecting the bottom of the closed curves on the fourth element to the top of the closed curves on the first element. Connect them with two bead sections using a flower bead cap, a seed bead, a 4mm bicone, a seed bead and a flower bead cap.

24 Sew half of the clasp to the second element and half of the clasp to the third element. Cover the back of the work with leather (page 29) to finish.

MANHATTAN
ring

FOR THIS RING, I CHOSE ELEGANT, CLASSY COLORS. These shades remind me of stars at night that are bright and deep in the heart of the city.

Approximately 1¼" × 1¼" (3.2cm × 3.2cm)

MATERIALS

soutache braids in three colors:

    A: black, 23¾" (60cm)

    B: metallic black silver, 15¾" (40cm)

    C: cream white, 15¾" (40cm)

1 Swarovski cosmic baguette flatback bead, 15mm × 5mm (jet)

5 Swarovski bicone beads, 3mm (jet)

3 Swarovski bicone beads, 4mm (sand opal)

20 rhinestones in a chain, 2.1mm wide (white opal)

1 ring base with a 15mm × 11mm pad (gold tone)

beading foundation (Lacy's Stiff Stuff)

leather or ultrasuede for backing

thread and invisible thread

embroidery needle

tape measure

scissors

glue

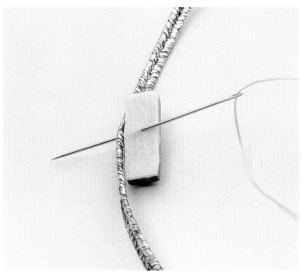

1   Glue the flatback bead to the foundation. When dry, cut around the bead. Cut a 3¼" (8cm) braid of each color. Thread the needle and cut the thread to a comfortable length and tie a knot at the end.

    Sew out from the center of one of the longer sides of the crystal bead and pass the needle through the middle of the B braid. Sew back through the braid to the foundation and keep sewing the B braid to this side of the crystal.

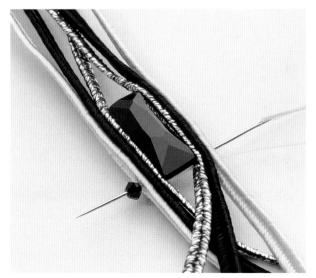

2   Sew on the A braid and then the C braid in the same way. Cut a 3¼" (8cm) braid of each color again and sew them to the other long side of the crystal. Pass the needle out from the base on the left side and pick up a 3mm bicone bead.

3 Bend the braids over the bicone bead and make a closed curve (page 20). Sew out on the opposite side of the flatback crystal and pick up a 4mm bicone bead.

4 Bend the braids over the 4mm bicone bead and make a closed curve around it. Create the same two curves on the other end of the flatback crystal using a 3mm and a 4mm bicone bead. Cut off the remaining braids and apply glue to the ends. Tie off the thread with several knots and clip close.

5 Cut one 4" (10cm) braid of color A. Thread your needle with invisible thread. Sew out at the stem of either 3mm bicone bead curve, then take the needle back, but do not pull the thread completely. Pass the first stone of the rhinestone chain through the loop and tighten the thread over the connection between the first two rhinestones in the chain. Continue attaching a total of ten rhinestones between the curve and the A braid (pages 21).

6 Repeat step 5 around the other 3mm bicone bead curve using the remaining ten rhinestones in the chain. Tie off the thread with several knots and clip close. Cut off the remaining braids and apply a thin coat of glue to the braid ends.

Cut one 8" (20cm) braid of color C. Thread the needle. Bend the braid in half and sew the bend between the two rhinestone curves.

7 Continue to sew the C braid around the two curves.

8 Sew the C braid completely around the two curves. Cut off the remaining braids and apply glue to the braid ends. Pass the needle through the braids of the flatback crystal, between the two rhinestone curves, and sew a 4mm bicone bead on top of the braids.

9 Cut a 4" (10cm) braid from colors A and B. Pass the needle through the braids at the stem of one 4mm bicone curve and stitch into the A braid and then the B braid.

10 Attach the braids to the top of the curve. At the end of the 4mm bicone curve, sew through the braids and pick up a 3mm bicone bead.

11 Make a closed curve around the bead. Repeat steps 9–10 around the other 4mm bicone curve.

12 Make a closed curve around the 3mm bicone bead. Cut off the remaining braids and apply a thin coat of glue to the ends.

Pass the needle up between the two 4mm bicone curves and sew a 3mm bicone bead onto the center top of the braids.

13 Place the piece onto the leather, trace around it and cut out the shape. Mark and cut two slits for the ring base, making sure the ring base will be behind the rhinestone part of the piece.

14 Insert the ring base through the slits, working from the back side of the leather, and secure it with a little glue.

Apply a thin coat of glue to the back center of the piece and attach it to the ring base. Then apply glue to the other parts of the leather and press carefully to the back of the piece.

TALOS *bracelet*

FOR THIS PIECE, I USED DARKER COLORS, and I've kept the design simple. However, the patina effect and the regular rows of tila beads give this bracelet an impressive look.

FINISHED SIZE

Approximately 7" (18cm)

MATERIALS

soutache braids in four colors:

    A: black, 51¼" (130cm)

    B: graphite gray, 45¼" (115cm)

    C: metallic black silver, 51¼" (130cm)

    D: silver gray, 23¾" (60cm)

Miyuki tila beads, 5mm, in two colors:

    A: matte metallic gray, 12 beads

    B: matte black, 9 beads

2 faceted rondelle beads, 4mm (jet)

3 faceted rondelle beads, 6mm × 8mm (jet)

15 Czech fire-polished beads, 2mm (jet)

1 Swarovski square fancy stone, 12mm (crystal black patina)

2 seed beads, 15/0 (black)

1 closed ring, 25mm (antique brass)

1 closed ring, 7mm (antique brass)

beading foundation (Lacy's Stiff Stuff)

leather or ultrasuede for backing

thread and invisible thread

embroidery needle

tape measure

scissors

glue

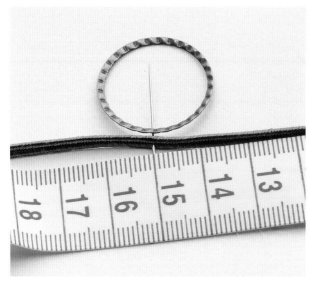

1 Glue the square fancy stone to the foundation. When dry, cut around the stone. Cut a 12" (30cm) braid from colors A, B and C. Thread the needle with invisible thread, cut the thread to a comfortable length and tie a knot at one end.

Start to attach the B braid to the 25mm closed ring (page 17), leaving a 6" (15cm) tail when you start.

2 Finish sewing on the B braid. Sew on the C braid and then the A braid. Sew all the braids together at the meeting point. Pass the needle up through the braids on the right side 1/8" (3mm) from the meeting point and pick up an A-colored tila bead. Bend the braids over the bead. Sew through the upper braids; at almost the same point, take the needle back through the braids and the bead.

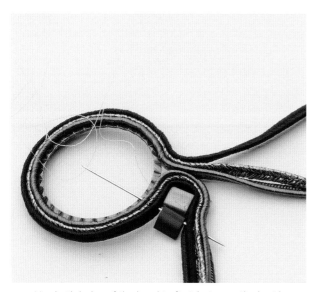

3 Use both holes of the bead to fix it between the braids. Sew a B-colored tila bead next to the A bead in the same way.

4 Repeat the A, B pattern with a total of four A beads and three B beads. Pass the needle through the outer hole of the last tila bead and pick up a 6mm × 8mm rondelle bead. Bend the braids over the bead and make a closed curve (page 20) around it.

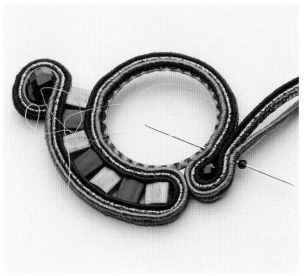

5 Lead the braids behind the tila beads and cut off the extra braids, then apply glue to the braid ends.

Lead the needle back to the meeting point and pass it up through the braids near the meeting point. Pick up a 4mm rondelle bead.

6 Bend the braids over the bead and make an open curve (page 19). Lead the needle slightly away through the braids of the base and sew the upper braids to the base at one point. Sew out from this point and pick up a fire-polished bead.

7 Make a closed curve around the fire-polished bead.

Still using invisible thread, fix the 7mm closed ring on top of the braids at the meeting point. Use several stitches to secure it. Tie off the thread and clip close.

8 Cut a 5½" (14cm) braid from colors A, C and D. Thread the needle. Sew out from the base under the curve from step 7 and stitch through the A braid.

9 Sew the braid approximately 1⅜" (3.5cm) around the base, then sew on the other two braids in the order D, C.

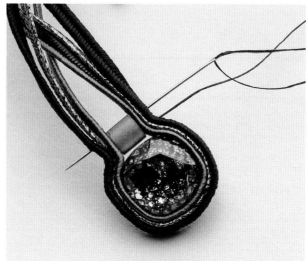

10 Pass the needle out at the last stitch and pick up a 4mm rondelle bead. Make a closed curve around it, then tie off the thread and clip close. Cut off the unnecessary braids and apply glue to the braid ends.

11 Thread the needle and cut an 8" (20cm) braid from colors A, B and C. Sew the braids around the square fancy stone with a closed wrap (page 15) in the order B, C, A. Sew an A-colored tila bead between the braids as shown.

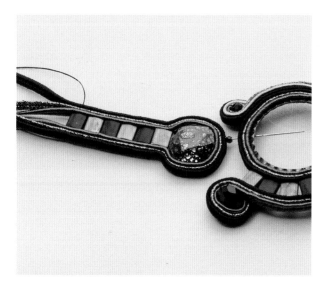

12 Sew on a B-colored bead, then continue alternating colors for a total of six tila beads. My bracelet is roughly 7" (18cm) long. Use more tila beads for a longer bracelet; use fewer beads for a shorter bracelet.

Sew out the top of the square stone roughly ⅛" (3mm) from the center. Pick up a fire-polished bead and stitch through the closed ring braids, roughly ⅛" (3mm) from the stem of the rondelle curve. Lead the needle under the closed ring and stitch back through the bead and farther down the base of the stone element.

13 Lead the needle over ⅛" (3mm) from the first fire-polished bead and sew on a second fire-polished bead to connect the two elements. Make several stitches to secure them. Tie off the thread and clip close.

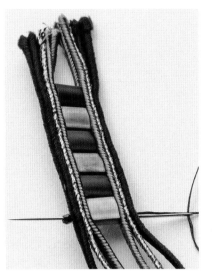

14 Thread the needle and cut two 4" (10cm) braids of colors A, B and C. Make two stacks of braids in the order A, C, B. Fix a B-colored tila bead between the B braids in each stack. Use both holes of the bead to fix it between the braids.

15 Sew on an A-colored bead. Continue to alternate the beads for a total of six beads, three of each color. For a longer or shorter bracelet, adjust the number of beads as you did in step 12. Sew out the last hole of the last tila bead and pick up a fire-polished bead.

16 Make a closed curve around the fire-polished bead. Repeat on the other side of the last tila bead. Cut off the unnecessary braids and apply glue to the braid ends.

Use two fire-polished beads to attach this element to the curves of the closed ring element as shown. Tie off the thread with several knots and clip close.

17 Cut two 8¾" (22cm) braids of each of the four colors. Align them and make two stacks of braids in this order: A, D, C, B. Make a hand-embroidered clasp (page 23), using two 6mm × 8mm rondelle beads and two seed beads on top of the braids, an A-colored tila bead between the braids, fire-polished beads above and below the tila bead between the braids and fire-polished beads for the curves.

18 Sew one half of the clasp to each end of the base. Cover the back of the work with leather (page 29) to finish.

MARGARET *brooch*

THE BLACK ONYX CABOCHON IS STUNNING, so all you need to do to complete this piece is pick some daggers and glass beads in your favorite color. You'll soon have an exciting piece of jewelry.

FINISHED SIZE
Approximately 3" × 3" (7.6cm × 7.6cm), excluding drop

MATERIALS

soutache braids in three colors:

A: metallic black silver, 53¼" (135cm)

B: claret, 69" (175cm)

C: dark gray, 53¼" (135cm)

1 onyx cabochon round flatback, 30mm (black)

4 Czech brick beads, 3mm × 6mm (luster opaque rose gold topaz)

2 Swarovski bicone beads, 6mm (jet)

2 Swarovski bicone beads, 3mm (rose opal)

1 Miyuki tila bead, 5mm (mustard yellow)

4 Czech dagger two-hole beads, 5mm × 16mm (luster opaque rose gold topaz)

2 Czech pressed-glass rice beads, 8mm × 6mm (jet)

12 rhinestones in chain, 2.1mm wide (jet)

2 Czech oval table-cut beads, 11mm × 9mm (pink coral brown picasso)

1 Czech druk round bead, 4mm (luster opaque rose gold topaz)

1 Czech glass twisted bead, 24mm (black antique gold)

1 faceted rondelle bead, 4mm (jet)

2 Czech druk round beads, 6mm (opaque pink and luster)

1 seed bead, 15/0 (matte bronze)

2 flower bead caps, 5mm (bronze)

1 brooch base, 33mm (bronze tone)

beading foundation (Lacy's Stiff Stuff)

leather or ultrasuede for backing

thread and invisible thread

embroidery needle

tape measure

scissors

glue

1 Glue the cabochon, the dagger beads and the oval table-cut beads to the beading foundation. When dry, cut around the beads. Cut two 12" (30cm) braids of color B and one 12" (30cm) braid of colors A and C. Thread the needle, cut the thread to a comfortable length and tie a knot at one end.

Pass the needle through the foundation of the cabochon and through the middle of the A braid.

2 Sew back through the braid farther down the foundation. Sew the first braid around the cabochon with a closed wrap (page 15).

Sew on the other braids in the order B, B, C. Sew the braids together at the meeting point with several stitches. Pass the needle out of the base and through the braids roughly $\frac{1}{16}$" (2mm) from the meeting point. Pick up a brick bead.

3 Bend four pieces of braid over the brick bead and sew through the braids. Sew back through the upper braids, the bead and the base. Fix this bead through the second hole in the same way. Sew on a second brick bead in the same way. Repeat by sewing two brick beads to the other side of the meeting point.

Pass the needle through the outer hole of the second brick bead. Pick up a 6mm bicone bead.

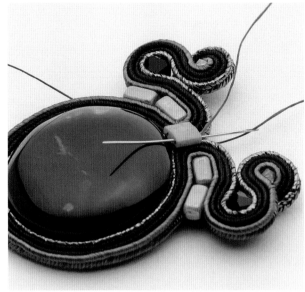

4 Bend the four braids over the bicone bead and make an open curve (page 19). Lead the needle slightly away through the braids of the base and sew to the upper braids at one point. Make a few stitches to secure. Sew out from this point and pick up a 3mm bicone bead.

5 Make a closed curve (page 20) around the 3mm bead. Lead the braids behind the work, cut off the remaining braids and apply a thin coat of glue to the braid ends. Starting at the second hole of the brick bead on the other side, repeat the curves around a 6mm and 3mm bead as described in steps 4-5.

Sew out from the meeting point about 1⁄16" (2.5mm) from the meeting point and sew a tila bead on top of the braids. Use both holes of the bead to secure it. Tie off the thread with several knots and clip close.

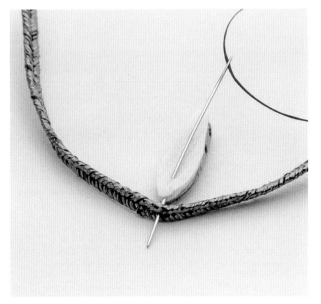

6 Thread the needle. Cut a 4" (10cm) braid of each color. Pass the needle through the foundation of one dagger bead and through the middle of the A braid.

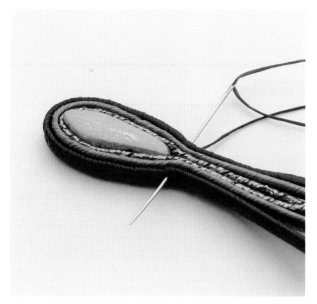

7 Make a closed wrap through the foundation and the bead holes.

Sew on the C braid and then the B braid. Sew the braids together at the meeting point with several stitches.

8 Stitch the dagger element to the base of the main element just above one set of brick beads.

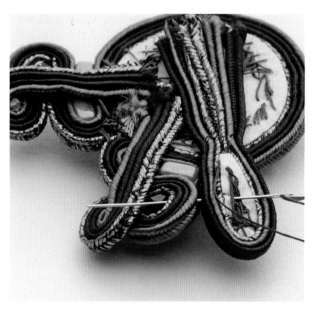

9 Stitch the dagger element to the 6mm bicone curve. Use several stitches to secure it and cut off the remaining braids. Apply a thin coat of glue to the braid ends and tie off the thread with several knots. Clip the threads close.

10 Repeat steps 6–9 to make and attach three more dagger bead elements. You should have two dagger elements on each side of the cabochon as shown.

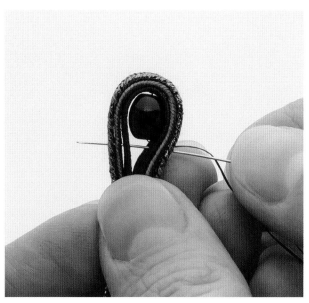

11 Thread the needle and cut a 4" (10cm) braid of each color. Make a closed wrap without beading foundation (page 16) around one rice bead using the braids in the order B, C, A. Repeat this step with the other rice bead.

12 Fix the two rice bead elements to the base under the dagger beads. Secure them with several stitches and tie off the threads.

13 Thread the needle with invisible thread. Cut a 6" (15cm) braid of each color. Sew the rhinestone chain between the two rice bead elements (page 21). Apply the braids in the order B, C, A.

14 Stitch the braids to one rice bead curve with several stitches. Pass the needle through the braids under the last rhinestone of the chain and pick up a 6mm druk round bead.

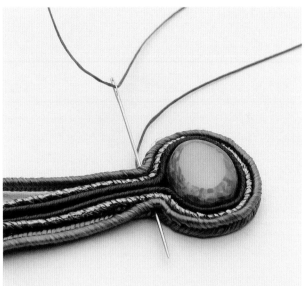

15 Make a closed curve around the 6mm round bead. Repeat step 14 at the other end of the rhinestone chain. Lead the braids behind the base, cut off the remaining braids and apply glue to the ends. Tie off the thread with several knots and clip close.

16 Thread the needle and cut 5¼" (13cm) braids of each color. Make a closed wrap around one oval table-cut bead using the braids in the order B, A, C. Sew the braids together at the meeting point with several stitches.

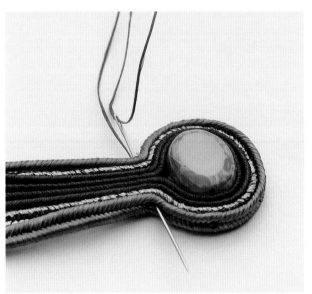

17 Sew the oval bead element to the top of the base between the two 3mm bicone curves. Secure it with several stitches to the base and to the curves.

Sew out from the meeting point above the tila bead and sew the rondelle bead onto the top of the braids. Tie off the thread and clip close.

18 Thread the needle. Cut two 5¼" (13cm) braids of color B and one 5¼" (13cm) braid of colors A and C. Make a closed wrap around the second oval table-cut bead using the braids in the order B, B, A, C. Sew the braids together at the meeting point with several stitches.

19 Sew this element to the bottom of the base, centered between the two druk round curves.

20 Pass the needle through the braids in the center bottom of the second oval bead element. Pick up the 4mm druk round bead, a flower bead cap, the glass twisted bead, a flower bead cap and the seed bead. Go back through all except the last seed bead. Secure them to the base several times and tie off the thread with several knots. Clip close.

21 Place the piece on the leather and trace around it. Cut out the shape and mark and cut two slits for the shanks of the pin back. Insert the pin back through the slits, working from the back side of the leather, and secure it using a little glue.

22 Apply a thin coat of glue to the back of the piece and press the leather carefully in place (page 29) to finish.

PALMA *pendant*

ALTHOUGH THE NUMBER OF SOUTACHE SHAPES are minimal, the bold focal piece and the unexpected details add depth and interest to this pendant.

FINISHED SIZE

Approximately 32¾" (83cm) long; pendant is approximately 4" (10cm) long, including drop

MATERIALS

soutache braids in four colors:

A: mustard, 33½" (85cm)

B: lime, 27½" (70cm)

C: old rose, 45¼" (115cm)

D: light brown, 39½" (100cm)

14" (35cm) leather cord, 2mm (brown)

1 Swarovski fancy pear, 40mm × 27mm (jet nut)

11 Miyuki tila beads, 5mm (matte opaque mustard)

1 Czech glass drop bead, 12mm × 8mm (milky coffee brown picasso)

38–40 rhinestones in a chain, 2.1mm (chalk white)

2 two-hole dagger beads, 5mm × 16mm (luster opaque rose gold topaz)

4 seed beads, 15/0 (opaque yellow)

5 Czech fire-polished beads, 3mm (opaque lime green)

1 Czech oval bead, 17mm (white ripple picasso)

1 felt bead, 12mm (light brown)

2 Czech faceted glass beads, 6mm × 8mm (opaque beige picasso)

8 Czech cathedral beads, 4mm (opaque dusky pink with bronze edging)

1 closed ring, 19mm (antique gold)

1 closed ring, 12mm (gold colored)

4 flower bead caps, 5mm (copper tone)

beading foundation (Lacy's Stiff Stuff)

leather or ultrasuede for backing

thread and invisible thread

embroidery needle

tape measure

scissors

glue

1 Glue the fancy pear to the beading foundation using the rivolis and pointed-back stone technique (page 10). When dry, cut around the stone. Cut a 12" (30cm) braid from colors B and C. Thread the needle, cut the thread to a comfortable length and tie a knot at one end.

Make a closed wrap (page 15) around the pear with the B braid, leaving a 3⅛" (8cm) tail.

2 Sew on the C braid and fix the two braids together at the meeting point. Make a few stitches to secure them. Tie off the thread and clip close.

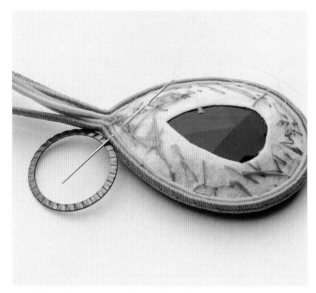

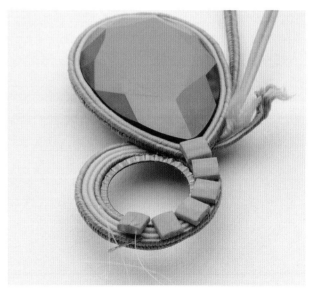

3 Thread the needle with invisible thread. Pass the needle through the braids on the left side (with the back of the piece facing up), roughly ⅛" (3mm) from the meeting point. Start to sew the braids around the 19mm closed ring (page 17).

4 Continue to sew all the braids around the ring. Lead the braid ends to the back of the work. Take the needle back to the meeting point, pass the needle up through the braids and sew a tila bead on top of the braids. Continue to stitch all 11 tila beads to the top of the braids around the closed ring.

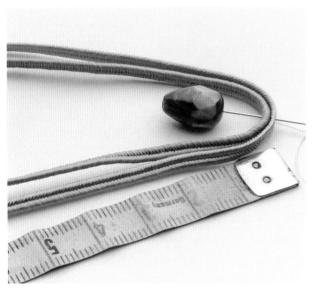

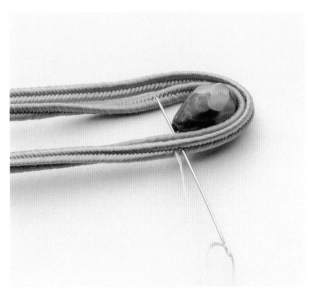

5 Cut a 10" (25cm) braid of colors A and C. Thread your needle with invisible thread and cut it to a longer length. Using the cover-the-knot technique (page 16, step 1), fix the two braids together 4¼" (11cm) from one end. Secure them with several stitches. Thread the needle into the A braid and pick up the glass drop bead so it sits next to the C braid.

6 Wrap two braids around each side of the bead. Stitch through the inner braids beneath the bead. Stitch up slightly from the previous spot, sew back to below the bead and go through the outer group. Don't pull the thread completely so you can add rhinestone chain in the next step.

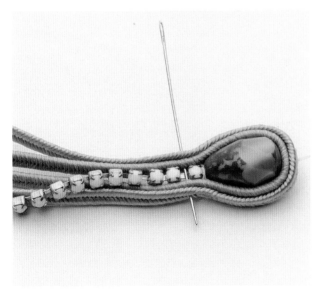

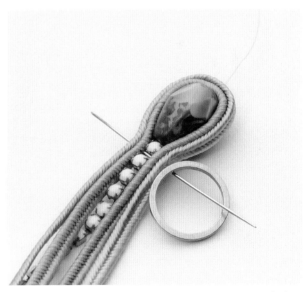

7 Lead the needle ⅛" (3mm) down either group of braids. Stitch through both braid groups, but don't pull the thread tight. Align the first rhinestone in the chain between the braids and sew back through both braid groups, over the connection between the first two rhinestones in the chain.

8 Stitch back through the braids at the same spot. With the needle exiting the right-hand braid, pick up the 12mm closed ring.

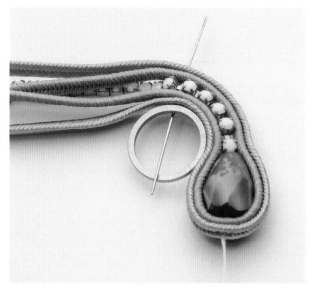

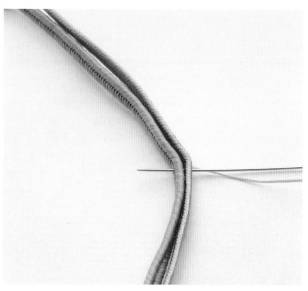

9 Attach the rhinestone chain between the braids (page 21) at the same time you attach the braids around the ring. Use fifteen to seventeen rhinestones to go completely around the closed ring, then lead the braids behind the bead.

10 Cut a 4" (10cm) braid of colors A and C and thread your needle. Stack the braids in the order A, C. Find the center, then fix the two braids together ⅜" (1cm) to either side of the center.

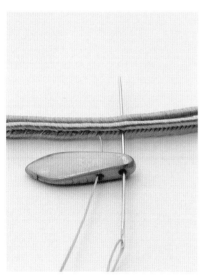

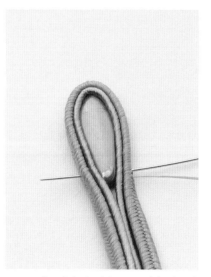

11 Stitch through the C braid to the A braid, then pass the needle through the lower hole of the dagger bead and stitch back through the upper hole, through both braids.

12 Bend the braids around the bead, fix them together through the holes and sew the braids together under the bead at the meeting point. Create a second element following steps 10–12.

13 Fix one dagger element to the back of the base under the closed ring. Attach the dagger element to the closed ring braids too.

14 Sew the other dagger element next to the first. Then sew the rhinestone element next to the second dagger, referring to the photo. Secure each element to both the back and the neighboring braids. Cut off the remaining braids and apply glue to the braid ends. Tie off the thread with several knots and clip close.

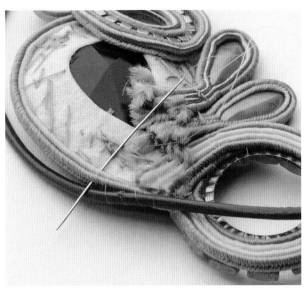

15 Thread your needle with invisible thread. Pass the needle through the braids on the empty side of the pear in line with the meeting point below the pear. Leaving a tail 4¾" (12cm) long, attach the leather braid by sewing out from the base under the leather braid and sewing back to the base over the leather braid. Do not sew through the leather braid.

16 When the leather braid has been sewn, lead the remaining leather braid under the drop bead element and bend it over the element, through the closed ring.

17 Loop the leather braid through the same element again.

18 Sew the leather braid end to the back of the work. Use several stitches to secure it to the base. Cut off the braid, tie off the thread and clip close.

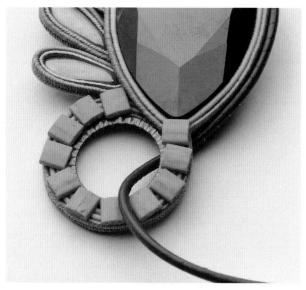

19 Lead the other end of the leather braid over the closed ring from below.

20 Bend the leather braid over the closed ring two times. With invisible thread, sew the braid end to the back of the work. Make several stitches to secure it to the base. Cut off the braid, tie off the thread and clip close.

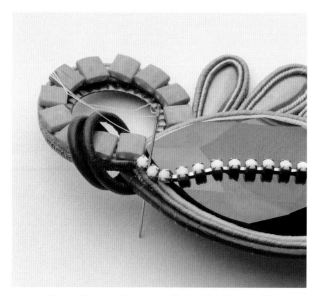

21 Thread the needle again with invisible thread. Bring the needle up through the braids below the leather and right under the tila bead closest to the tip of the pear. Take the needle back down at almost the same point, but don't pull the thread completely. Place the first rhinestone of the remaining rhinestone chain through the loop and tighten the thread over the connection between the first two rhinestones in the chain. Attach the rhinestone chain to the top of the braids round the pear.

22 When you reach the drop bead element, sew the remaining rhinestone chain to the top of the drop bead element braids as shown.

23 With invisible thread, pass the needle out at the bottom of the drop bead element in line with the top of the bead. Pick up a seed bead, a 3mm fire-polished bead, a bead cap, the oval bead, a bead cap and a seed bead. Go back through all the beads except the last seed bead. Fix them to the bottom of the base with several stitches.

Sew out from the base roughly ⅜" (1cm) from the drop bead element. Pick up a seed bead, a flower bead cap, the felt bead, a bead cap and a seed bead. Go back through all the beads except the last seed bead. Fix them to the bottom of the base with several stitches.

24 Cut a 23¾" (60cm) braid of color D and bend it in half. At the bend, fix it to the back of the opposite end of the base. Sew it to the stem of the closed ring near the two leather loops. This is the pendant's chain.

25 Cut two 8" (20cm) braids of each color. Align the braids and make two stacks in this order: B, C, A, D. Make a hand-embroidered clasp (page 23), using two 8mm × 6mm faceted beads on top of the braids, 4mm cathedral beads between the braids in a diamond shape (page 28) and 3mm fire-polished beads for the curves.

Sew half of the clasp to each end of the pendant chain.

26 Cover the back of the work with leather (page 29) to finish.

resources

BEADS, FINDINGS AND SUPPLIES

Nirvana Beads
26 Janis St.
Hudson, NY 12534
(518) 697-7547
www.nirvanabeads.com

Koralex s.r.o.
Alšovice 156
468 21 Bratríkov
Czech Republic
(420) 777 991 991
www.czechbeads.eu

Bead & Trim
357 W. 36th St.
New York, NY 10018
(212) 725-9845
www.beadandtrim.com

SOUTACHE

The Beadsmith
37 Hayward Ave.
Carteret, NJ 07008
(732) 969-5300
www.beadsmith.com

index

www.fwcommunity.com

20 19 18 17 16   5 4 3 2 1

Distributed in Canada by Fraser Direct
100 Armstrong Avenue
Georgetown, ON, Canada L7G 5S4
Tel: (905) 877-4411

Distributed in the U.K. and Europe by F&W MEDIA INTERNATIONAL
Brunel House, Newton Abbot, Devon, TQ12 4PU, England
Tel: (+44) 1626 323200, Fax: (+44) 1626 323319
E-mail: enquiries@fwmedia.com

Distributed in Australia by Capricorn Link
P.O. Box 704, S. Windsor NSW, 2756 Australia
Tel: (02) 4560 1600 Fax: (02) 4577 5288
E-mail: books@capricornlink.com.au

SRN: T5933
ISBN-13: 978-1-4402-4374-5

Edited by Christine Doyle and Noel Rivera
Designed by Clare Finney
Production coordinated by Jennifer Bass
Photography by Mihaly Kovacs and Csilla Papp

METRIC CONVERSION CHART

To convert	to	multiply by
Inches	Centimeters	2.54
Centimeters	Inches	0.4
Feet	Centimeters	30.5
Centimeters	Feet	0.03
Yards	Meters	0.9
Meters	Yards	1.1

ABOUT THE AUTHOR

Csilla Papp was born and raised in Hungary, where she made beaded animal figures and Christmas decorations as a child. In school, she studied cinematography and literature and later moved to England with her husband and two beautiful daughters, Hanna and Emma.

In England, she started beading again while raising her children. In January 2011, she made her first beaded creations using peyote stitch, and then she slowly learned other techniques. She tried beadweaving and bead embroidery, and although she loved them both, she felt there was something missing from each. She then came across soutache and immediately knew she had to try the technique. She has been exploring ways to combine soutache with beadweaving and embroidery ever since.

Csilla's work has been published in *Digital Beading Magazine* and *Beads & Beyond* magazine. She teaches across the United Kingdom and writes and sells tutorials and finished jewelry online. She recently moved back to Hungary.

ACKNOWLEDGMENTS

A very special thanks goes out to my family for the support they provided me as I worked on this book. I must acknowledge my husband and best friend, Misi, without whose love, encouragement and assistance I would not have finished this whole process.

Thanks to my parents and my brother for everything they gave me, and thank you for always supporting me and believing in me.

A big thank you to two good friends, James Kevin Barker and Norma Barker, for the love and constant support they have given me throughout the years. Even though we're far apart, you're always in my heart.

Thank you to Amelia Johanson for finding me and providing the opportunity to write this book, and a special thanks to Noel Rivera for your support and enthusiasm.

Thanks to the F+W Media team members who worked on this book. I could never have done it without you!

Thanks to those artists who have inspired me and supported me along my beading journey.

MORE GREAT *jewelry titles*

SOLDERED ALCHEMY

24 Jewelry Projects Using New Soft-Solder
Techniques

LAURA BETH LOVE

For too long, solder has been an afterthought in
jewelry-making—used only for bezels and connec-
tions—but not anymore! In *Soldered Alchemy*, you'll
learn new, creative ways to make solder the star-
ring element of your jewelry. Twenty-four gorgeous
projects with detailed photos walk you through the
basics of decorative solder, bridging wire with solder,
adding copper or vintage patinas and more.

MASTERING TORCH-FIRED ENAMEL JEWELRY

The Next Steps in Painting With Fire

BARBARA LEWIS

This follow up to the award-winning *Torch-Fired Enamel
Jewelry* combines the beauty (and ease!) of torch-firing
enamel with creative jewelry and metalsmithing techniques. Inside, you'll find more than fifty techniques for
enameling, metalsmithing, beading and wireworking, and
seventeen step-by-step projects, including necklaces,
earrings and bracelets. You'll also get more than fifteen
new color "recipes," plus advice for layering enamels, and
a contributor gallery highlighting work with specific color
concepts.

Find more fantastic jewelry books, magazines and projects in our online stores!

VISIT WWW.INTERWEAVESTORE.COM FOR MORE DETAILS.
